THE PRESIDENCY IN BLACK AND WHITE

THE PRESIDENCY IN BLACK AND WHITE

MY UP-CLOSE VIEW OF FOUR PRESIDENTS AND RACE IN AMERICA

April Ryan

Foreword by the
Honorable Elijah Cummings

ROWMAN & LITTLEFIELD
Lanham • Boulder • New York • London

Published by Rowman & Littlefield
A wholly owned subsidary of The Rowman & Littlefield Publishing Group, Inc.
4501 Forbes Boulevard, Suite 200, Lanham, Maryland 20706
www.rowman.com

Unit A, Whitacre Mews, 26-34 Stannary Street, London SE11 4AB

Distributed by NATIONAL BOOK NETWORK

British Library Cataloguing in Publication Information Available

Library of Congress Cataloging-in-Publication Data
Ryan, April, 1967–
  The presidency in black and white : my up-close view of four presidents and race in America / April Ryan.
    pages cm
  Includes bibliographical references and index.
  1. Presidents—United States—Racial attitudes. 2. United States—Race relations—Political aspects. 3. Clinton, Bill, 1946—-Relations with African Americans. 4. Bush, George W. (George Walker), 1946—-Relations with African Americans. 5. Obama, Barack—Relations with African Americans. 6. Presidents—Press coverage—United States—History—20th century. 7. Presidents—Press coverage—United States—History—21st century. 8. United States—Race relations—Press coverage. 9. Ryan, April, 1967- 10. African American women journalists—Biography. I. Title.
  E176.472.A34R93 2015
  305.800973—dc23

                                                    2014033007

ISBN 978-1-4422-3841-1 (cloth edition)
ISBN 978-1-4422-3842-8 (electronic: cloth edition)
ISBN 978-1-5381-0663-1 (paperback edition)
ISBN 978-1-5381-0664-8 (electronic: paperback edition)

∞™ The paper used in this publication meets the minimum requirements of American National Standard for Information Sciences—Permanence of Paper for Printed Library Materials, ANSI/NISO Z39.48-1992.

Printed in the United States of America

This book is dedicated to the loving memory of my mother,
Vivian Ryan, to my father, Robert Ryan Sr.,
and my brother, Robert Ryan Jr., and
last but not least, to my two daughters, Ryan and Grace.

HABAKKUK 2:2–3

² *And the LORD answered me, and said,*
Write the vision, and make it plain upon tables, that he may
run that readeth it.
³ *For the vision is yet for an appointed time, but at the end it*
shall speak, and not lie:
though it tarry, wait for it; because it will surely come, it will
not tarry.

CONTENTS

FOREWORD

The Honorable Elijah Cummings

O black boy of Atlanta!
But half was spoken;
The slave's chains and the master's
Alike are broken;

The one curse of the races
Held both in tether;
They are rising—all are rising—
The black and white together.

John Greenleaf Whittier

I have begun this brief preface to *The Presidency in Black and White* with an excerpt from Whittier's nineteenth-century poem to emphasize an insight about our rapidly evolving and increasingly diverse twenty-first century society. Either our children will inherit a nation that offers universal opportunity and a truly "color-blind" respect for the dignity and potential of every American—or they will face a far more problematic destiny.

April Ryan's window into presidential decision making on racial issues offers grounds for both optimism and concern. Her first-person observations of the four Presidents she has covered on a daily basis have value for all Americans, whatever may be our ethnic heritage. Americans need to know far more about the decisions that each President has made in addressing the challenges of racial division in our country, as well as those opportunities for progress that they have missed. *The Presidency in Black and White* offers a compelling "insider's" exposition on both points. The author does so in the context of a very personal narrative of her own journey behind the veil that, all too often, hides the humanity of our leaders—and those who report upon them—from the citizens whom they serve.

I have been listening to April Ryan's reports and commentary on Baltimore radio for longer than either of us might comfortably acknowledge, longer even than her seventeen-year sojourn as a distinguished member of the White House Press Corps. I have paid attention to what she has to say because she is a serious and insightful journalist who works very hard to fulfill the three cardinal duties of a free press in our democratic republic. She is truthful, carefully distinguishing between the objective facts that she is reporting and her opinions about what those facts should mean to her audience. She is tenacious, willing to dig below the surface to give her audience something closer to the whole truth. Equally important, I have found her reports to be consistently relevant, offering her audience news that is useful to the better-informed public that is the ultimate foundation of any successful democratic republic.

All three qualities are reflected in this penetrating chronicle of the events of our time by a capable reporter who was thrust into the center of American political power at an early age. For any woman (especially a young Black woman representing the "specialty" urban press), April Ryan's challenge has been a daunting one. Her story of perseverance and ultimate success is inspiring.

Above all else, however, April Ryan's chronicle is a very human one, told with the same honesty and compassion (as well as criticism) that she affords to the three leaders whom she has closely observed for nearly two decades. When we consider the Presidents whom we elect to guide our nation and the most complex government in the world, we tend to forget that they are human beings attempting to do an almost impossible job. *The Presidency in Black and White* reveals the relationships between our Presidents, who need to maintain public support for their policies, and a female Black journalist, who both reports to a too often ignored audience with legitimate and longstanding concerns and is herself a member of that minority.

For the White House reporter, the key consideration in those relationships has been achieving access to the Presidents that she needs to do her job. For the Presidents, and for those who serve them, the principal objective, necessarily, has been one of political leverage. Their respective priorities are often in conflict, but in our system of government, both access to information and the political leverage required to achieve a more equitable society are necessary.

Far too many Americans are struggling today, Americans of color most of all. For our struggles to succeed—for us to all rise together, as John Whittier dreamed—we need to fully utilize the democratic power of our growing numbers. We can no longer expect our Presidents to be magicians, miraculously applying executive power to correct every wrong and further every aspiration. We are better served by viewing our Presidents as our chief architects and engineers, retained by a large and unruly family to repair the house that we share.

April Ryan's long service in the White House Press Corps has given her an intimate understanding of the value of political leverage, for Presidents and the American public alike. "Give me a place to stand, and I shall move the World," the Greek mathematician and engineer, Archimedes of Syracuse is said to have asserted in demonstrating the principle of the lever. *The Presidency in Black and White* is an important contribution toward achieving that political leverage—that place for us to stand from which we can move our nation toward the society it is meant to become. For that, April Ryan deserves our gratitude and support.

ACKNOWLEDGMENTS

Thank you, American Urban Radio Networks, for providing me with this unique perch for almost twenty years.

Thank you to Ron and Judy Davenport for your support that put this entire journey in perspective. Mr. Davenport, from the beginning you said, "Close my eyes that I might see." I have been following the formula for the vision.

To Jerry Lopes, it has been a great roller coaster ride. Let's keep breaking news and setting the pace.

A special thank you to all those who participated with on-the-record quotes for this project: it means so much as people rarely like to go on the record for anything in Washington, D.C.

To Samantha Ible, thank you for your make-up artistry always, be it for TV, the White House Correspondents' Association Dinner, or this book cover. You are the best! ible4makeup@gmail.com

To Diane Nine, the literary agent of all agents who never gave up on this project as it was years in the making. You made it happen! Your insight is why we are here today! I am so thankful for you. To Dave Smitherman, you are so witty and simply amazing. This team rocked, and I could not have done this at all without you! You are wonderful!

Rowman & Littlefield, thank you for believing in my vision and making my dream the reality it is today. I cannot express how much I appreciate you, Jon, for having the guts to tackle this project, and to the rest of the Rowman & Littlefield family, I am grateful for your support.

To Norman Hall, thank you for encouraging me from day one to journal and write my White House story.

To Valerie, you support the vision. For that I am eternally grateful. The fabric of America at its best. You are indeed the best!

To my incredible friends who have supported me, stood by me, wiped my tears, and listened to me in good and bad times. Whew, we made it. You all have kept the positive thoughts and words going to give me inspiration to move forward with this book.

To my very large family. My mother would be so pleased. I love you and thank you for loving me back in each way you have. It is a very special love and bond we share!

To my Aunt Pearl who has been there since my birth. You have been my rock. I could not have fulfilled this dream if you had not loved me and my kids.

To my baby brother! Robbie, I love you tremendously. You started this all by lending me your office without hesitation in the early morning hours to begin writing this book. Now it is done. We did it!

To my father. You have given me the courage to speak truth to power as you have done all my life. Thank you, and I love you.

To my late mother! You encouraged me to keep writing when times were not the best. You encouraged me from my infancy that I could do anything I put my mind to with hard work. Even though you are not here, we completed this project.

To my children, Ryan and Grace, you are my heroes and continue to inspire me every day to do more and be a better person. God has blessed me tremendously with the love and care of you two. I am so thankful for you both. Mommy loves you both. Ryan and Grace, you don't have to ask any more if I am finished writing my book. Here it is! Ryan and Grace, this book is for you to understand you both can do anything.

INTRODUCTION

It was my biggest Christmas present ever—I had just landed the ultimate job for any news reporter—the White House beat. It was a perfectly clear December evening, and the sky looked like a deep indigo velvet carpet that had been strewn with twinkling diamonds. It was unusually cold for Washington, D.C. in December, and each time I exhaled, my breath formed large clouds around my head. Despite the brisk air, I was oblivious to anything but the scene in front of me.

As I gazed at the beautiful, white mansion through the poles of the tall, black metal fence, I was transfixed by its stately facade and gently leaned my head against one of the poles, letting out a gentle sigh as I did. At that moment, a warm feeling of pride, patriotism, and affection washed over me and made me forget about the cold. The portico of the White House's entrance is easily recognized by even young schoolchildren, and people come from around the world to admire its handsome lines.

The simple white stone is in stark contrast with the black, wrought-iron carriage lamp that is suspended by a heavy, metal chain. This iconic entrance is the perfect backdrop for holiday greenery and deep red ribbons, and when lit up at night, it glows like a beacon. The White House is a grand two-hundred-year-old building that so embodies architectural symmetry and elegance that I think only the most confirmed cynic could resist its charms.

So much of our history, national pride, and sense of patriotism are wrapped up in the White House that the thought of going to work there made my heart skip a beat. It hadn't really dawned on me until now that in a matter of weeks I would be working at the White House! As I leaned against the cold fence, tears started slowly streaming down my face. It took me a minute to realize that it wasn't the cold wind making me cry—these were tears of joy, excitement, and maybe a bit of nervousness.

Up to this point in my career, my broadcast experience had included thirteen years as news director at an AM/FM radio station in Baltimore; and a gig hosting and producing a public affairs show on cable. From time to time I freelanced as an anchor for WTOP, one of the AM radio stations in Washington, D.C., but I certainly had never been a political reporter, unlike most of my White House colleagues.

As if all of this weren't intimidating enough, the man I was replacing had been in the position for almost two decades and had been the head of the White House Correspondents' Association. I was filled with joy, fear, and trepidation at the prospect of filling his shoes, and I asked myself, "Could I make this work? Would I be able to earn the same respect as other veteran White House reporters I'd seen on television? Would the President ever call on me by name at press conferences?" Later, after two years on the job, the answer to each question turned out to be a resounding "yes!" But only after a few bumps along the way.

Knowing how things work inside the Beltway as I do now, my fears at the White House beat were somewhat warranted. A reporter at ABC Television once told me, "It is a different league here in Washington because the stakes are so much higher. . . . The players inside the Beltway must be skilled. The ones that aren't are thrown out."

Now that the moment I'd been waiting for had finally arrived, all I could do was stare at the White House. It was still hard for me to believe that a working-class Black girl like me from Baltimore was going to be covering the most powerful seat of government on Earth. My eyes were still filled with tears as I asked myself the same question over and over again, "How did I get here?"

Officially, I wouldn't start working at the White House until January, but that didn't help ease any of my anxiety. This was a huge step in my career, and I was deeply grateful for the chance to cover the President. Washington power politics hadn't jaded me, so I had immense respect for the institution and the Office of the President, unlike many of my colleagues in the media.

My wide-eyed awe of the White House may have pegged me as a newbie, but who wouldn't be intimidated? Access to power is the real currency in Washington, and it's easy for people on the inside to lose sight of the city's special place in our government, in American history, and in world history. Most Americans have some inkling of the pomp and power of the presidency from watching television shows like *Scandal*, *House of Cards*, *The West Wing*, and from movies such as *The American President*. As President Clinton's Press Secretary, Mike McCurry, said about Washington power: "Power is the ability to shape and influence events, to bend history in one direction or another. Some actors have

~~greater power than others, but anyone who can bend that arc of history has the most important thing in Washington—currency and relevancy."~~

And there is nothing like being an insider to really feel the effect of the presidency. That's when you get to see history being made. To feel that power from the vantage point of the West Wing is a political junkie's dream, and it offers a rush like no other. Working at the White House is the ultimate insider's job in Washington, and Mike McCurry paid me a great compliment after I began my new beat: "There is no question to me that your reporting demonstrated that kind of power."

But for me it's more than just power and status. Everything about the place is enthralling, including the building's architecture. Photographs just don't do it justice. It's physically imposing, both inside and out, and it is a testament to our early leaders' understanding of the importance of creating an imposing and symbolic presence. To be successful, the members of our young nation would need powerful physical symbols to instill confidence and a sense of pride. They instinctively knew that we needed to establish our legitimacy and convey to the rest of the world that our nation was strong. And that required more than just rhetoric. It called for a physical presence that would show the world that the new nation wasn't just made up of backwoods frontier men who lacked education and sophistication.

This desire to impress is evident in James Hoban's architectural design, which gives the elegant stone building an almost regal air. The vast grounds include eighteen acres of majestic gardens, lawns, and groves. Since its construction in 1792, the White House has succeeded in becoming much more than just the home of Presidents and their families. It has become the symbol of democracy and freedom, the very cornerstones of our country. The sad irony is that this great house, like the Capitol and many of the historic buildings in Washington, was built with slave labor.

Many Presidents brought slaves to live with them as cooks, housekeepers, personal maids, and servants in the White House. In fact, the second child born at the President's House, as it was called then, was a child born to Thomas Jefferson's slaves, Fanny and Eddy. The White House Historical Association notes that the first African American to write a memoir about the White House was Paul Jennings, a slave, who was President Madison's personal servant. His book, *A Colored Man's Reminiscences of James Madison*, offers a detailed, firsthand account of what a slave's life was like at the White House. Jennings is also credited with helping to save the portrait of George Washington as Dolley Madison's slave when the White House burned down. The White House Historical Association research shows that later, during both President Andrew Jackson's and President Polk's times in office, slaves were brought to live at the White House and were often housed in rooms located in the basement.

This was actually a common practice since many of our former Presidents were from southern slave states. Later, when President Lincoln freed the slaves and slavery was abolished, he refused to have slaves at the White House, but Blacks were still relegated to service positions on the household staff. As broadcaster Tavis Smiley told me:

> "For years [African Americans] have been the butlers, the maids, the kitchen help, the maintenance help. So Black folk . . . have always had access to the White House . . . just in areas where they were invisible. And now we have Negros in the White House in more visible ways. For those of us who can just go in through the front door and enter visibly, it has a way of seducing us. The nature of the building is always fascinating to me."

The White House is the epicenter of what has been called the most powerful city in the world, and it has been a thrill for me to work there for more than eighteen years. One thing I can say for sure is that my job never gets boring. Even a slow day at the White House is exciting because being there gives you a front-row seat to history in the making, especially if you're a reporter. For staffers, it's the chance to be an integral part of history, so none of us ever take it for granted. I never lose sight of how lucky I am to be there.

Seasoned journalist veterans also feel this way. Helen Thomas, former Dean of the White House Press Corps, covered the White House longer than anyone else in history, and her tenure included ten Presidents. As she said, "I think that I am just very, very lucky to cover history every day. When it is not happening, it is going to. You always have a sense of anticipation, because everything comes to the White House, one way or another, from the most trivial story, or seemingly so, to war and peace."

What makes my take on race relations and the presidency so unique is my perspective. I am the only Black woman reporter with a permanent press pass whose audience is urban America. Despite tremendous strides in discrimination based on race and gender, I work in a White, male-dominated power structure that doesn't always like to make room for people who are different—people who look like me. Over the years I have seen Presidents, staffers, and other reporters come and go, and each administration has a chance for a new beginning and to make real strides when it comes to the racial divide. Of course, not every President has actually made race relations a priority, but it's my job to evaluate each of their performances for my audience.

Like many others, I thought that the election of our first Black President would be a great opportunity to expand the audience for this important dialogue on race. So I wrote this book for all Americans, not just for Black Americans. As Congressman James Clyburn (currently the third-ranking Democrat in the House of Representatives) told me, "I think it's one of the problems we have politically today, of people who just seem not to want to have an honest discussion of race. That is keeping this country from getting where it ought to be, because we won't have that serious discussion." It is my hope that by revealing how race is handled at the White House, we can evaluate if they have gotten it right, and if not, decide what it is we want and need them to do differently.

This book is told straight from the heart. It includes honest discussions that may be construed by some as politically and racially charged or divisive, but that's not what I set out to do. My goal is to encourage people to start talking honestly about race. I want this book to be a catalyst for communication so that we can finally begin the process of reconciliation, healing, and possibly even reparations. We need to hold our past, current, and future leaders accountable and get them to put our interests at the forefront, without focusing on how it may affect their legacy or their chances for reelection.

Slavery and discrimination are not just part of our country's ugly past; they continue to influence how Whites and Blacks deal with each other. Of course, they especially permeate every aspect of Black people's lives in one way or another. I want to initiate the discussion on race, not lead it. I leave that task to our leaders; they are much wiser and far more experienced in policy and analysis. If we are to change how we deal with issues of race and the relations between Whites and Blacks, however, Americans of every background need to be proactive and play a part in bearing witness to the truth.

None of us can afford to leave the decision about who sets the agenda to politicians alone. If we have learned anything from our nation's history, it's that our defining moments have often been the result of our ability to work together in harmony to achieve great things. Not long ago, Americans, despite our differences, cast aside the yoke of segregation and took a stand for freedom. If we could do that in the midst of chaos, turmoil, violence, and fear, then certainly it's worth continuing the work begun just a few decades ago.

As Blacks, we have to stop seeing ourselves as hyphenated Americans or symbols of a tragic past and collectively assert that we can achieve Dr. Martin Luther King, Jr.'s dream. Not in the future, but now. To do this, everyone, not just Black folks, has to think about what race means to them. The Black community needs to move forward and do the work too, by voicing *our* opinions on which race-related issues get put on the national agenda. We can't just leave it up to White folks and politicians. That's not fair to anyone. Barack Obama's historic election as the first Black U.S. President was the apex of a unique convergence of conditions that compels—no, demands—that Black folks define what it means to be Black in America and what legacy we want to leave for our children.

Americans are decent people at heart, but we have to have the courage to trust that, as a nation, we are capable of confronting the shame of slavery and racism and the stains they leave on our hearts. We have shied away from the wrenching ugliness of our racist history for far too long. In the past, race has been a lightning rod for misunderstanding and dissension. Many have responded by pushing the issues aside for fear of the torrent of emotions and turmoil that they might unleash, not to mention politicians afraid to potentially upset their constituents.

Our nation and government, specifically the President, must offer a sincere apology for the evils of slavery and the crippling legacy of segregation and discrimination that still oppresses Blacks in every sector of society. Americans must atone for the damage that has been done to generations of slaves and their descendants, spiritually, psychologically, and financially. Before we can come together as a nation and resolve the pressing issues caused by racism, our government must take responsibility for its part in the systematic injustices that have historically been heaped on Black people based solely on the color of their skin.

But we must go further. Yes, an apology will begin the healing process, but many believe reparations can truly repair the damage done, help to even the economic playing field, and begin to bring closure to an open wound that has been festering for centuries. When Randall Robinson, the great human rights activist and founder of TransAfrica, was asked why reparations were necessary in an interview by Amitabh Pal for *The Progressive* magazine's October 2005 issue, he put it best when he said, "It's important for White America to be able to face up. Far beyond its relations with the Black community, it is important for White Americans. It's important in helping us in our approaches to the rest of the world, and in being sensitive to Islam, and to look at the way other cultures handle their management of themselves, and to look at it with respect, with the possibility that you even might learn something. We've got a country that never takes any responsibility for anything. It forgets its role and makes everybody else forget what happened, too. And that it is not just dangerous for the victim, but also for the perpetrator."

The inevitable discussion can't be ignored any longer; the presidential election of 2008 confirmed that for everyone. The time is ripe for a sea of change in race relations, and this change can and should be led by the one person in this country most qualified to speak with empathy and personal conviction about the issues of race—the President. Who else can we trust to carry the weight of our nation's history on their shoulders? It may not be fair to saddle a man already heavily burdened by the dual challenges of war and financial calamity, but if not him, then who, and if not now, then when?

This book does what others have failed to do—it delivers the real story on race at the White House. My questions, research, and in-depth interviews with our leaders have all been driven by my sincere wish to get the dialogue started. I have struggled to report on the issues that affect urban communities and have avoided clouding my reporting with hidden personal agendas. I have put questions and issues about race front and center at White House press conferences, rather than let them become an afterthought in the minds of the administration. Whenever the White House has tried to side step or avoid the issues, I have pointed this out, much to the chagrin of whoever is sitting in the Oval Office at the time. It would be much easier for me to just maintain the status quo and not rock the boat, but then I wouldn't be doing my job. I have a responsibility as a woman of color, with access to the most powerful people in the world, to ask tough questions and push them for solutions. Frankly, there's no one else in a position to do it. The fact that we have twice elected a President of mixed heritage is not enough.

But I wouldn't have been able to do this without access and assistance from some "inside" players. Either by permission or through attribution, these key players have shared their thoughts on race with me. Their insights and wisdom have provided the background information that makes it possible for me to do my job. I want to assess the White House's lack of involvement in the lingering controversy of race relations. I don't purport to be an expert on race or a sociologist, but what I can tell you is that I have created my own report card for each President, and I'll share those with you later in this book. I have tried to discuss the issues related to race and give them context. By reviewing how they have been handled in a broad sense, we can better evaluate each President's performance and decide for ourselves what work still needs to be done.

Besides Paul Jennings's memoir, few Black writers or reporters have chronicled race relations or the Black experience at the White House. As the first Black woman accredited to cover Congress and the White House, Alice Dunnigan's autobiography, *A Black Woman's Experience: From Schoolhouse to White House*, chronicled her life, but also her groundbreaking work as a reporter at the White House. She is not alone, and her work is joined by two other important books: *Black Man in the White House: A Diary of the Eisenhower Years by the Administrative Officer for Special Projects, the White House*, penned by E. Frederic Morrow in the 1950s, and *Bill Clinton and Black America* written in 2002 by Dewayne Wickham, columnist for *USA Today* and the Gannett News

Service. His book cites, but not from a firsthand perspective, my experience putting together a soul food dinner for President Clinton that was attended by many prominent Black journalists.

As a reporter for urban radio, I am in what's called the "specialty media" category. Usually, we aren't given the same kind of access as major networks, but because my niche is urban news it can often give me an entrée or make me stand out in the minds of our leaders, including the President.

Over time, I have succeeded in getting racial discrimination, poverty, poor housing, unemployment, HIV/AIDS, lack of good education, inequality in the legal system, lack of economic opportunity, and many other issues important to urban listeners before the President. Because there are so few reporters covering this beat, and because these pressing issues can also have national impact, I am often the "go to" person in White House briefings when there are questions about race. It's this unique perch that convinced me that I am suited to tackle the subject of race relations in the White House.

In this book, I share my experiences in the White House as well as my interviews with some of the most powerful people in our country's history. I feel it's my obligation to myself, my audience, my community, and my daughters to shed light on the things I've seen and experienced throughout my career. It's my hope that these issues will get the attention they rightly deserve, because in the end, it can only help us grow as a nation.

As Abraham Lincoln said, "No man is good enough to govern another man without the other's consent." We certainly gave these leaders our consent by electing them, but that doesn't mean our involvement stops there. As far as I'm concerned, it's my job to help make sure the voices of urban America are heard.

Change begins here. When it begins is determined by the President.

ESTABLISHING A
RACIAL BASELINE

When they have abolished slavery, the moderns still have to eradicate a much more intangible and tenacious prejudice— the prejudice of race. Differences [between races] have lasted for centuries, and they still subsist in very many places; everywhere they have left traces which, though imaginary, time is hardly able to obliterate. I see slavery is in retreat, but the prejudice from which it arose is immovable.

—Alexis de Tocqueville, 1865

Before I tell you about my first days at the White House and my exciting journey into the world of Capitol Hill journalism, it's important to set the stage as far as the current state of race relations in this country and more specifically among influential Washington power players, as I have observed so far. When I began covering politics, I didn't know exactly what to expect, but what I heard and learned from the many interviews I have conducted was quite surprising.

I believe on some level I thought most of these cultured politicians and lawmakers would somehow have a different outlook on diversity and racial equality. Maybe it was naiveté on my part, but because these people are so educated and well traveled, I expected a more enlightened view of the topic. Perhaps I was being optimistic or maybe just overly hopeful, but after being in the White House and reporting on stories for many years, I have discovered that we still have a long way to go before we are truly a country united.

To thoroughly test my theory of a racial divide in our nation's capital, I set out to interview many different people, from high-powered politicians to business executives and thought leaders. I wasn't sure if I would be able to secure meetings with all of the people on my wish list, but I was determined to give it the historic-Black-college try. And I was pleasantly surprised when almost everyone I approached agreed that the topic is an important one, and they were willing to share their views. To me, that in itself shows that we are ready for change and that we can move forward when it comes to such a difficult, complex issue.

Before I share some of those thought-provoking discussions, it's important to talk about what has happened in the past because of racism and inequality. Unfortunately, every Black person I spoke with had many personal stories about how their own family had been so negatively affected by racism and hate, all stemming from our history of inequality and persecution. As a race, we were never able to establish a level playing field, never had a chance to compete and be judged on the same terms as White people. While those who are not directly affected can decide not to think about the unfortunate past, it's something Black folks are reminded of almost every day.

Bishop T. D. Jakes, senior pastor of the Potter's House and CEO of TDJ Enterprises, told me the shocking story of his grandfather's murder at the hands of White men. His grandfather worked in the logging industry in the rural area of Hattiesburg, Mississippi, in the 1950s. In order to get home from his work site, he often walked across a field and swam through a lake. On June 9, 1957, this hard-working Black man had an argument with some White men. Later, when he jumped into the lake to swim across to meet his pregnant wife, he was ensnared by barbed wire placed in the lake by those men. He was trapped under the water, bled profusely, and drowned. Jakes's grandmother was left pregnant and widowed in her early twenties.

What is it about human beings that makes one race think it is superior to another just because the color of its skin is different? If anthropologists, sociologists, psychologists, and all the other "-ologists" out there could answer this, we might be able find a way to end this scourge. Unfortunately, racism is a part of the human experience, and it's not just limited to White-on-Black hatred. Humans seem to have an incredible capacity for hurting each other. None of us is immune. I have discovered that even perceptive, well-educated people can hold ignorant, irrational aversions to a particular race and teach this kind of value to their children. What other reason could there be for racism's strong hold on our country for so long?

As Bishop Jakes says, "I think the thing most devastating is not the racism that I've experienced, or that my ancestors and predecessors have experienced.

What was most painful was to raise my children and notice them going through various forms of racism today. One of (my sons) is light-complected, and the other one is dark. I said (to the lighter-skinned child), 'When I was your age, I was about your complexion, but as I got older, I got darker.' And he started crying."

Jakes asked the child what was wrong. He said, "I don't want to be dark like my brother." Jakes asked the boy, "Why?" He said, "The darker you are, the more they dislike you!" The boy was in elementary school. As Bishop Jakes told me, "It was apparent to me, if a six-year-old is encountering (racism), then God help the rest of us."

Racism and discrimination have overshadowed our country and our people since the first slaves were brought to America against their will from Angola in 1619. Their treatment at the hands of barbarous traders and White owners opened the door to a history that many would like to forget, and one that included the genocide and mass enslavement of millions of Africans. For more than *two hundred years*, slavery was a legal reality that allowed Whites to buy and sell Black people at will and treat them like nothing more than chattel. Slaves in America were subjected to violence on an order heretofore seen only in the Spanish conquistadores' genocidal attacks on Native Americans. The Bill of Rights and the U.S. Constitution aside, the human rights of my ancestors and most other Black families' ancestors were ripped away and violated in a virulent form of moral and political hypocrisy. The result was that racism became part of America's national heritage that we refused to even teach about in school.

From the very beginning, slave traders, owners, and pro-slavery advocates belittled Blacks, made the argument that they were incapable of taking care of themselves because they were inferior to Whites, that they didn't really want to be free, and that they were physically better suited to hard labor. By constantly dehumanizing Black people, the slave trade used fear and ignorance to perpetuate false racial stereotypes and ethnic myths, many of which still exist today. The more Blacks were portrayed as less than human, the easier it was to look the other way at what was being done to them.

The widespread growth of racial terrorist groups like the Ku Klux Klan (KKK) and White supremacy organizations after the defeat of the Confederacy made sure that Blacks were kept down even after they were freed. These groups used intimidation and violence even after slavery was abolished, and they succeeded in stifling White sympathizers or anyone opposed to slavery from openly speaking out for fear of retribution. These terrorist groups and the politicians who opposed the Republican Reconstruction successfully made most of the South, the border states, and parts of the North impossible places for Black people and businesses to live and prosper on a level equal to what others enjoyed. This went hand in hand with the spread of myths and stereotypes that only served to reinforce many of the false and ignorant generalizations that kept Whites and Blacks divided.

Because slavery stripped Africans of their humanity, that made it easier to justify what was done to keep them bound to a life of inhumane servitude, and the more beaten down the slaves were, the easier they were to control. By taking away any hope of salvation, freedom, or sense of human dignity, the slaves were too downtrodden to rebel and overthrow their masters. Every shred of personal autonomy and identity was denied them. Even their given birth names were taken from them and substituted with ones chosen by slave traders or their masters. In many cases, further damage was inflicted when slaves were forced to take the surname of their owners, as if they were an extension of the property or plantation.

To further subjugate and demoralize them, slaves weren't allowed to practice their religion, and they were stripped of their culture and language. Any connection to their home and families back in Africa was severed, and the use of psychological torture was employed to keep slaves emotionally and mentally vulnerable. The slavers and owners thought nothing of breaking up families and selling mothers, fathers, and children to different owners. Torn apart, without any idea of their destination, many families were separated and never saw each other again. This may even somehow relate to today's all-too-often reality of the broken Black family, where the mother is the sole caregiver and a strong male presence is nowhere to be found.

This systematic shackling of minds and spirits helped keep slaves from organizing in large numbers, and it prevented any large uprisings or overthrow of the power structure. Many times, escape was a death sentence, and those who helped them escape or hid them were given the same harsh punishments. Each succeeding generation of slaves born under the yoke of oppression was further and further removed from their patrimony and eventually became lost souls bereft of any comforting link to family or heritage. The agony of loss, separation, fear, pain, loneliness, and despair must have been overwhelming, and it was certainly debilitating.

While President Lincoln's Emancipation Proclamation is lauded for setting free the slaves in rebellious states that had been a part of the Confederacy, it didn't abolish the physical and psychological torture that made the horrors of slavery real in the hearts and minds of slaves, their children, and their descendants. The Thirteenth Amendment's moral tone and lofty goals often rang hollow in former slave states in the South as the insidious specter of Jim Crow spread across the former Confederacy like a pestilence. While slavery may have been abolished in theory, in practice, the country was still a dangerous place to live for Black people, and freedom was an artificial construct that was reserved for Whites.

In many parts of the country, a host of conditions helped keep any wholesale ability to fight for freedom at bay. The cards were stacked too high against them. The various levels of government played their role in helping keep Blacks down, but it was the state governments in the South that kept Blacks from really being free. Jim Crow laws and a perfect storm of conditions made living conditions after slavery almost as unbearable as slavery had been. Debilitating, draconian share-cropping practices, White violence, lynchings, the terrorizing of Blacks and Black businesses by the KKK, widespread bigotry, and government sanctioned or initiated discrimination all kept Black folks separate and isolated.

Jim Crow's "separate but equal" policy was based on hatred, ignorance, and fear. The concept of "separate but equal" was, of course, never truly equal. It was a twisted, sinister lie perpetuated to keep Blacks down for yet another hundred years. These state laws institutionalized racism and essentially legalized bigoted attitudes and the violence that came with them. No matter where they went, but especially in the South, Blacks were relegated to the status of second-class citizens. They were prohibited from sharing schools, hospitals, public transportation, drinking fountains, restaurants, theatres, clubs, and restrooms with Whites. This segregation turned ordinary people into rapacious bullies and harbingers of violence, and as a result, bigotry became a pervasive evil whose filth left no area of our society untainted.

I am grateful that I did not have to live in the same America that my parents, grandparents, and ancestors did. Although racism is still present today, I cannot imagine life as a slave or living in a segregated society. It's a wonder how Blacks survived the insanity for so long without losing their minds. Although I am too young to have lived in the era of segregation, I have felt the fear and outrage of being subjected to the kinds of indiscriminate, senseless acts of violence and terrifying intimidation that were part of segregation's legacy. I remember one incident clearly, because I can still feel the sheer terror of that moment in the pit of my stomach. It was the first time I ever thought that being Black could get me killed.

I was just a little girl at the time, and I was visiting my grandparents out in the country. My grandfather had about one hundred acres of land, which for a Black man back then was a lot of land, and he lived at the end of a long, winding road. His house was so far down this road, anytime you saw someone on the road you didn't know, you knew that they weren't supposed to be there. One day I saw a

CHAPTER 1

ll of White people heading down toward my grandfather's place.
ched the house, they lifted up rifles and aimed them at the house where we were. I thought that I would die from fright, and couldn't imagine why they wanted to shoot us; we hadn't done anything to them. Suddenly, instead of shooting, they yelled in my direction and thankfully turned around and left, inflicting no physical harm but giving a young girl quite a scare.

Even though I was only a child, at that moment I realized how difficult life must have been for my parents, grandparents, and their parents before them. What is so sad is that this kind of thing has been repeated thousands of times, and often with much more tragic consequences. It's all part and parcel of the Black experience in America. I had heard about slavery growing up, and had read about its toll on Black people, but I had no emotional understanding of what it really meant.

I finally came face-to-face with the harsh realities of slavery when I traveled to Africa with President Clinton in March 1998. This fateful trip would be life changing for many of us, and it proved historic for President Clinton. After planning for close to five years, President Clinton wanted to make this trip so he could personally offer a token of his friendship to the African nations working to become part of the world stage.

The official reason for the trip was to promote democracy, human rights, and economic development on a continent that chronically had been overlooked by most American Presidents. At the time, it was the longest trip of Clinton's presidency, and he would be the first American President to visit countries such as Uganda—making the trip historic on several levels.

An ancient and common reality crashed against the elite descendants of African slaves, as powerful, moving, and chilling as the equatorial currents nearby. Of varying skin tones, they were all visibly shaken from the sudden reopening of emotional wounds from the same dark past, four hundred wearying and mournful years of slavery and its aftermath. It was March 1998. A few members of the Congressional Black Caucus emerged from a tour of an unassuming brick structure on a dirt-covered, dead end street. While their dark sunglasses masked their eyes, they could not camouflage the tears that flowed that day on Goree Island. Their silence spoke witness of the palpable residue of brutality and torture inflicted on their innocent forbearers. Their mind's eye saw haunting spirits of a horrific past, dank dungeons aboard wooden ships that were nothing more than floating hells. They stood frozen with the thought of countless immobile bodies shackled on an arduous journey across steel gray seas, to a distant land, a new land they could never claim as home—and that would offer no respite to their suffering.

The lingering ghosts from the tyranny of that dreaded trip begged for closure to a chapter that blemishes America's history, if not its soul. A year before, in the summer of 1997, President Clinton's Initiative on Race had made headlines by considering the possibility of a government apology in the form of a resolution to soothe the unfathomable pain of hundreds of years of brutal, involuntary servitude. Ironically, the request for a congressional apology came from a White member of Congress, Democrat Tony Hall of Ohio. What a pleasant surprise! This is something our ancestors could have never imagined. Hall proposed a congressional apology for slavery to Americans of African descent. The matter immediately expanded to an even bigger issue, an apology from the Oval Office.

The timing for such action was considered advantageous because of the calm political waters. President Clinton was just into his second term, and there were no risks or dangerous pitfalls for tackling the issue. Normally the matter of race, particularly apologies for past American sins, is considered divisive enough to possibly end the career of a novice politician and would-be statesman. Yet the issue wasn't even prickly to the storm-weathered skin of this seasoned politician of more than two decades. After all, Clinton had volunteered to initiate an effort to heal the racial divide in America, which he considered a national curse. His obviously hopeful—if not simplistic—remedy was to call for a change in attitudes. He called for a celebration of cultural diversity, the varied ingredients of the so-called melting pot of America.

From the onset of the initiative, those outside the White House publicly questioned how the President could deal with the issue of bringing all races together by overlooking one of the nation's oldest racial fractures, failure to acknowledge the wrongs of slavery. Among healing words offered by Washington politicians, "sorry" or "apology" were not a part of the lexicon.

The possibility of an apology also drew contention within the Executive Mansion. Doubters, primarily staffers, erected the major stumbling blocks. They felt Clinton had already focused too much on African American issues, and they believed an apology wasn't part of the equation for his race initiative. There was also friction among those who shared his vision of racial harmony. This group of staffers wanted to broaden all discussions on race to include Native Americans, Asians, and Hispanics. They cited as evidence discrimination in the court system and overall economic disparity. Among some Black senior staffers, there was a belief that their White counterparts were discounting the struggle of their ancestors. Faint rumblings of that skirmish were floating around the Press Corps. (Believe me, rumors and gossip spread among the press like wildfire, even at the White House.)

Despite the varying opinions, senior staff and advisors told me emphatically that an apology would not happen. The swaying in the White House, pro and con, Black and White, would ultimately cause the President to vacillate on the issue, putting an apology for slavery on indefinite hold. Many Blacks in the nation were crying out for an apology, and even hoped that it would be the precursor for reparations. Long a nation of unrelenting stalwarts, an emergent groundswell was developing of those bold and hopeful enough that America could finally admit her wrong and even make restitution. It was reasoned that the wounds were inflicted so deeply that they remained not only unhealed but also infected.

For some it was no longer a stretch, because Clinton, a son of the racist South, had offered previous apologies to the survivors of the amoral Tuskegee syphilis experiment and to the human guinea pigs subjected to a government cereal radiation experiment. In 2010, Secretary of State Hillary Clinton and Health and Human Services Secretary Kathleen Sebelius also apologized to the government of Guatemala for an experiment conducted from 1946 to 1948 in which American public health doctors intentionally infected Guatemalan prisoners, mental patients, and soldiers with venereal diseases. The "experiment" was meant to test penicillin as a treatment for the diseases.

Even so, President Clinton's asking for forgiveness on behalf of the United States' role in the enslavement of Africans in America seemed unlikely to happen at this point. An insider at the White House told me that there were some who felt that the President didn't need to make so many apologies, especially because slavery had occurred so long ago. The ray of hope was that apparently others thought the issue should stay on the table.

Another reason why this seemed possible was because discussions had been initiated between Black farmers and the White House, which ultimately led to a meeting between the group and President Clinton. President Clinton began the process for the approval for monies to be awarded and paid to Black farmers in what was referred to as the "Pigford Settlement."

Back in 1997, a Black farmer from North Carolina named Timothy Pigford filed a lawsuit against the U.S. Department of Agriculture citing racial discrimination. He claimed that Black farmers were discriminated against because of race and thus were denied loans crucial to sustaining their farming businesses. This could be traced back to when the slaves were freed and Whites feared that they would be direct competition. The government made U.S. Department of Agriculture (USDA) loans dependent on a farmer's credit, which instantly put newly freed Blacks at a disadvantage.

Timothy Pigford was joined by four hundred other farmers in their pursuit of justice for what had always been an unlevel playing field where Blacks couldn't compete equally. The *Pigford* case helps to demonstrate how the sitting White House occupant plays a key role in reparations. The case was filed under the Clinton Administration, but eventual payouts came about under the Bush Administration, which did not share the same views. So while there was victory in the clear decision that restitution was owed, fulfilling that judgment proved challenging. A whopping 69 percent of the eligible claims were denied, and it was decided that almost 75,000 claims were received after the established deadline and thus denied, regardless of their merit. Finally, in 2014, over fifteen years after the initial case was filed, many farmers received payments, which for most equaled around $50,000.

This example demonstrates the important role of the White House when it comes to issues like reparations and restitution. Even if a favorable judgment is handed down, government red tape can make payment very difficult. Of course, during the fifteen years, which spanned the Great Recession, Black farmers still had to find a way to keep their farms going in order to provide for their families and their communities. And even when they did finally receive their monies, $50,000 is not a life-changing sum.

When I talked to Dr. John W. Boyd Jr., a farmer and civil rights activist and founder of the National Black Farmers Association (NBFA), he told me that he saw many changes to the proposed settlement throughout the various administrations.

"I filed my first complaint against the USDA in 1984. Since then, I have seen a lot of things happen both good and bad. In 1994, I began protesting against the USDA's discrimination of Black farmers by using the familiar 'forty acres and a mule' slogan to bring attention to the plight of the Black farmer. In 1997, we filed the Black farmers' lawsuit. I met with then-President Bill Clinton who settled the case; the Department of Agriculture with its ugly, racist head filed motions in federal court to deny the Black farmers class notification. From 2000 to 2008 I lobbied Congress to have the Black farmers' case reopened. At the time, then-Senator Obama was the lead sponsor of my bill and Senators Joe Biden and Ted Kennedy were cosponsors. With their support, the bill passed in May of 2008 and became a part of the Farm Bill."

Prior to the 2014 settlement, Boyd said, "The Obama Administration does not want to deal with the issue of race, and I find it very discouraging for Black America. The Black farmers are being dissed by the Obama Administration due to the simple fact that the Black farmers are a race-based issue. It seems that the administration wants nothing to do with us . . . but Black farmers were a popular issue during the campaign."

The apology issue really came to a head during President Clinton's historic six-nation trip to Africa in 1998. Accra, Ghana, the first tour city, is said to have been pivotal. Even for equatorial Africa, it was an unseasonably hot 106 degrees the day Clinton arrived in Ghana. A massive brown throng of untold thousands braved the relentless heat to see one of the most recognized men in the world. They were so excited to see this important man from America. The frenzied crowd ignored security warnings and came within arms-length of each vehicle traveling in the presidential motorcade that zipped anxiously through the streets of the West African city. Although the topic of a slavery apology was divisive, word was that discussions were "cordial." While the issue remained an ongoing story in the United States, most of the aides on the ground in Ghana and back in Washington persuaded Clinton not to say the two words he had said previously in official apologies: "I'm sorry."

Because Clinton did not seek federal forgiveness during the stop in Ghana, some thought he would avail himself of other opportunities by the time of the last stop in Dakar, Senegal. On the last leg of the tour, the most moving moment of the trip was a tugboat ride away from Dakar at one of the most heart-wrenching historical sites anywhere. The most powerful and freest man in the world visited Goree Island's slave house and the Door of No Return. For millions, the door marked the exit from humanity to chattel property. And for many others, it was the beginning of a doomed voyage. Only the strongest, or those who willed to live, survived the cramped and waste-strewn rooms of the slave quarters and the months-long rigor of the transatlantic crossing. *Maison des Esclaves* invoked emotions from all who walked through the wooden doors to tour the site with President Clinton. The curator spoke graphically as he showed us the pristine captain's quarters, and then the contrasting sodden holes where hundreds of slaves were kept like tormented beasts. We were told that women thought to be virgins were chosen for the voyage by the fullness of their breasts. Many of the virgin captives preferred rape as a way out of going to the new land. Ultimately, many of the women became pregnant. Their captors felt such women were tainted for breeding purposes.

After hearing the horrors and sharing the exact same space with such evils, the Black reporters on the trip were inspired to hold hands and share a united prayer. There, the four of us stood, African and American, telling the story and feeling the past, on a dock outside the Door of No Return. Could our prayer be original or one often repeated? Our petition to the divine was a plea for the freedom of any spirits separated from uprooted ancestors who, no doubt, also sought intervention from above. Our White colleagues saw the emotion and showed genuine concern for our confrontation with pain, unabated by time. The then-NBC radio correspondent Peter Maer and I stood on the dock at the same time, both filing reports. We finished recording our stories at about the same time. He extended his hand and gently placed four smooth, oblong rocks into my brown palm as a memento of what proved to be a mind-altering and life-changing experience. It was a gift I will always keep to remind me to never forget the day, or the past.

Like the Black reporters on the trip, emotions were present just beneath the typically strong veneer of those members of the Congressional Black Caucus who had accompanied the President and First Lady Hillary Rodham Clinton that day. Ostensibly, their dark glasses were to block out the direct rays of the equatorial sun. Their emotions were tapped and given voice by the Reverend Jesse Jackson, Clinton's Special Envoy to Africa.

Jackson offered a prayer with a group of lawmakers who were also affected by their witness of evil's abode and the ever-present realization of its aftermath on their constituents. After the tour, President Clinton emphasized how members of the delegation had climbed their way to become elected leaders in America, and they now stood in a land where their ancestors had departed as slaves. Those words were delivered just before he left the continent, and it was a powerful backdrop for offering an apology for slavery.

While the possibility of an apology had been one of the focal points of the twelve-day trip, at least one participant on the trip felt attention on Clinton was misdirected. During the third stop in Cape Town, South Africa, California Congresswoman Maxine Waters opined that an official apology shouldn't have come from the forty-second President. She bluntly suggested that a good candidate for the chore was Senator Jesse Helms of North Carolina. Given the internal division and debate on whether an apology was appropriate and over the responsibility for rendering national amends, Clinton seemingly had a reprieve.

What appeared to be heartfelt awareness in Africa apparently became lost to Clinton after the trip. A few months later in Washington, he delivered the keynote address at the White House Correspondents' Association Dinner. He showed his disregard, and likely mirrored the invisibility of the issue in the American psyche. He indirectly referenced the issue of a slavery apology. In what failed as lighthearted and inside humor, Clinton apologized for pineapple pizza and disco. It was cheap and camp, and at the expense of African Americans, the people James Baldwin said have their history recorded in the hieroglyphics of back scars. The attempt at humor achieved its aim. Guffaws from well-heeled and connected White attendees demonstrated amusement at supposed wit that disregarded the slavery experience. It also sent a message on the status of the issue in the Clinton White House that it could be fodder for a night of frivolity. President Clinton ultimately left office January 20, 2001, without saying, "I'm sorry."

Before leaving, Clinton wanted the onus of not apologizing for the enslavement of Africans in America taken off his hands. The only way to do that was to conduct a study on the effects of an apology. He gave the matter to the race commission. It never took action. According to documents available at the Clinton Library from 1997, the President's Initiative on Race (PIR) certainly entertained the possibility of an official apology. The PIR was made up of eleven different "working groups," among them Policy, Communications, Enforcement, Recruiting Leaders, Promising Practices, Tough Messages, and Dialogue in Communities. The goals of the PIR were to:

1. develop national policy initiatives,
2. recruit leaders and encourage efforts aimed at bridging racial divides in local communities across the country, and
3. raise the issue of racial reconciliations to the national agenda through dialogue.

In the "June Progress Report Qs&As," one of the questions was, "Why didn't the initiative deal with the apology for slavery issue?" And the response proved evasive. "The reaction to a formal apology reflects how deeply this issue continues to reverberate emotionally for a lot of Americans, both black and white. However, the initiative has made a serious effort to expand the racial dialogue beyond issues of black and white. One objective of the initiative was to move the country towards recognizing and realizing the full potential of its diversity. We have done that by finding ways in which we can offer real opportunities to Americans who work hard, but who continue to face barriers of discrimination based on race."

So Clinton was just as indecisive on the matter as the opinions he received from those he consulted. Some wanted economic empowerment, and others wanted the fleeting words, which could have led to actual reparations. A heated disagreement also divided the Congressional Black Caucus. Some fought vehemently for economic empowerment, while others fought just as hard for an enunciation of regret. Jesse Jackson was in the economic empowerment camp. There was also a split among the ranks of Black staffers at the White House. That was more crippling than anything else. When no one else could penetrate the bubble that surrounds the inner sanctum, they had the President's ear on a daily basis.

Some who knew Clinton thought he had the insight and wisdom to see Blacks have been severely wronged throughout history. One tangible indication was a gift he presented to his former White House attorney and defense team star, Cheryl Mills. The then thirty-three-year-old Black attorney's brilliance was credited in part for a successful defense against claims that Clinton violated the civil rights of women who accused him of sexual advances. As a token of his appreciation for her work, Clinton presented Mills with a copy of the controversial book *The Slaughter: An American Atrocity*. It details the killing of 1,200 Black Army soldiers in 1943. The book's author contends that the perpetrator was the U.S. Army. Author Carroll Case compiled the work after investigating years of rumors about massacres. The book describes the U.S. Army's alleged killing of the soldiers on a base in Mississippi and states that the soldiers' families were told they died overseas in battle during World War II. Part two is fictional but based on accounts compiled during Case's probe. Because of the book's detailed accusations, the U.S. Army conducted its own probe. After their investigation into the published allegations, the Army formally stated the accounts of Carroll Case's book were not true. The President gave Mills the book months before the military even began its investigation.

Why would a sitting White President of the United States give a Black attorney a book that purports conspiratorial government racial atrocities in the Deep South? Mills thought the gift was appropriate and indicative of the President. She knew him in a much different way than most Americans. They interacted as coworkers and friends on an almost daily basis, forming a bond as attorney-client and as friends.

The take on Clinton's racial sensitivity is positive from those outside his authority as well. Former Maryland Congressman and National Association for the Advancement of Colored People (NAACP) President, CEO Kwiesi Mfume believes he has a vantage point for judging Clinton on race. "I served under three Presidents, and yes, I can see a clear distinction in the way all three have dealt with minority issues. For Ronald Reagan, there was no such thing as a minority issue. He, in some of his own remarks, said that he really didn't see what the problem was. We had a President who was pretty much blind to the fact that there was a growing minority community nationwide of Blacks and Latinos and Asians, and no real sense that their issues needed attention." Mfume's assessment of Reagan's successor is not much better. "With George H. Bush you have a President who in some respects was not blind, but often times had blinders on." Mfume offers high praise for Clinton, "a son of the South who has a different sort of background, who relates differently to people of color, and who has not been afraid to express that. That doesn't mean that he is without criticism in his whole issue of minority outreach, but it certainly means that he has done far more than anyone else." As for tangible results, Mfume thinks Clinton made a difference. "In ten years, I have seen change, real change." He cautioned, "It's not just a matter of having come a long, long way, it is still a matter for us of having a long, long way to go."

While one would expect Mfume, a former Democratic Congressman from Maryland to be kind to Clinton, a similar assessment is offered by a Republican politician and unsuccessful White House aspirant who now calls Clinton a friend, admits the GOP has a spotty record on race. "On the Republican side, we have got miles to go. If we are going to be a national party we have got to get a bigger umbrella. That is one thing that Clinton has been able to do. He has been able to sort of move to the middle where most people are, regardless of race or gender or whatever." The politician credits Clinton's inclusion efforts with changing how future Presidents will deal with minorities and the underprivileged.

Given his publicly stated focus on the significance of "building bridges," why didn't Clinton start the path to healing with an apology? Later, he did share some of his insights on the topic.

The occasion was a soul food dinner prepared by my Aunt Pearl in the summer of 1999 that was organized by the Black correspondents and attended by Clinton. The menu was typical of more festive events. It included chitlins, fried garlic chicken, black-eyed peas, collard greens, and cornbread. Among the potluck items brought by my colleagues were barbecue ribs and peach cobbler. Clinton was casual in his conversation, attitude, and attire in the off-the-record event. He did make a formal statement, responding to the question about why he never apologized for slavery.

He said, "Some of the problem in the Black community is that African Americans do not come together on issues." The forty-second President of the United States dared to say something that is secretly uttered in White circles, and openly debated by Blacks. The room filled with Black reporters and two White House staffers sitting at a long wooden dinner table were taut with anticipation for his next candid statement. During a brief pause following the stinging words, I couldn't help but interrupt him with the rhetorical question, "Did you all hear that? A President of the United States made that comment."

Because so many Black people consider him "the first Black President," he got away with that statement. Truthfully, he is one of the few White men unofficially granted license to make such a comment. Perhaps it is because his supporters, of varying colors, believe his concern for racial healing is genuine, that he ironically didn't feel the need to apologize for the remark, or for government-sanctioned slavery.

When I interviewed Bill Clinton for this book, I asked him where he sees the current racial climate in this country. He replied,

"Much of the world today is still struggling to be born as a Democratic, just, free place in many places. If you look at the time it took America to even get close to getting the race question right, we were born as a country that enshrined slavery in the Constitution and counted African Americans as six-tenths of a person for purposes of the census. Ironically, the antislave states wanted to keep down the number of Southerners from Congress since they knew African Americans couldn't vote. So you had a guy like Thomas Jefferson who said when he thought of slavery he trembled to think 'God was just.' But he never freed his slaves, unlike George Washington."

But what did he think about how other administrations, particularly that of his predecessor George H. W. Bush, handled racial equality in this country?

"I disagree with his economic policy, but I never thought it was a race-based policy. I don't think he would be discriminating against people . . . I think their whole economic policy is wrong because it basically increases poverty and doesn't create enough jobs. But, I think he believed it and I think the reasons he supported it had nothing to do with race. This racial polarization is a thing of relatively recent event-age. Gerald Ford, remember, was on an integrated football team at the University of Michigan. There was still some Abraham Lincoln left in the Republicans for a long time until then basically it started in the 1980s getting away from them. One thing I always liked about Bush is that he talked to anybody."

I was a bit surprised by his answer when I asked him why he chose to participate in the soul food dinner.

"You invited me. You'd be amazed how many times people never invite people, once they get to be President, to do anything on a human scale. I mean, you get invited to lots of fund-raisers and dinners and asked would you come speak. I am talking about going out to dinner and talking. You would be amazed how little it happens. Even now to me it barely happens."

Slavery and its aftermath has economically, physically, emotionally, and psychologically damaged generations of Black Americans and built up a subculture composed of negative stereotypes, myths, ingrained beliefs, and hereditary bigotry. This organized system has destroyed the self-esteem and sense of worth of people of color for far too long. As Reverend Jesse Jackson said,

"Today, African Americans and the poor are facing some devastating conditions. Disparities are getting wider. We are number one in athletics, number one in presidential politics, and also number one in infant mortality. (We are) number one in short life expectancy, number one in housing discrimination, number one in home foreclosures, number one in the prison industrial complex, number one in low graduation rates, number one in the victims of the subprime lending scam and schemes."

Discrimination has kept Blacks from earning fair wages, getting good educations, and getting fair trials. It has violated their human and constitutional rights, kept them from owning property, forced them to live in substandard housing, deprived them of access to quality medical care, created a separate society where poverty and joblessness are the norm, destabilized families and social relationships, and diminished hope. All of these conditions have subjected Blacks to a centuries-old version of post-traumatic stress disorder that has kept Blacks down while lifting up Whites.

Racism in America has shown that we are capable of the basest of human behaviors. Slavery, lynchings, the KKK, rape, violence, genocide, torture, segregation, and a lack of legal freedoms—these should not be the words a free and democratic people use to describe their experiences as citizens. These are the words we often use to describe lawless dictatorships led by mass-murdering terrorists like Hitler or Stalin, not life in a democracy. And yet they are a part of Black folks' lexicon as much as the Declaration of Independence and the Constitution. America has been culpable in this travesty of justice, and yet we still do not, as a nation, want to atone for what we have done.

Is it any wonder, then, that there is still animosity in the Black community toward some who still harbor pre–civil rights era mind-sets? We can't afford the luxury of trust when it comes to this country's historic power structure. We have lived without it for so long that we cannot willingly turn our backs on history for fear of the repercussions. We won't be betrayed again by Whites in the interest of political expediency.

Time and again, we have counted on politicians and civil rights leaders to bring about change and ease the pain of racism, only to be told, "Wait. The time isn't yet right. We need to take small steps." During the early Obama years, music mogul and CEO of KWL Enterprises Kevin Liles told me about a time he was invited to sit with President George W. Bush during Black Music Month. He said, "Whether Republican or Democrat, I wanted a seat at the table. I wanted open discussions around the war on poverty we should be fighting, around the war on poor education we should be fighting, and the war on entrepreneurship and innovation that we are lacking in this country. It's never going to be about Democrat or Republican; it's always about what is right and wrong."

Well, we are tired of waiting for the "old guard" to do what is right by us, and we do need a seat at the table. The laws to protect us are in place. We now have a Black man in the Oval Office, and we aren't going to give a pass to candidates and politicians who go back on their campaign promises. We also aren't going to let politicians ignore race or sweep the issues under the rug. Rainbow Coalition President Jesse Jackson told me, "Those who supply the pressure and leverage get heard. If you have a good case, you'll prevail. First, you've got to be heard; then you can prevail."

Dr. Jeffrey Gardere, Assistant Professor, Behavioral Medicine at Touro College of Osteopathic Medicine in New York City, had an interesting, if not optimistic, outlook on possible changes in behavior and thought among one of the most important Republicans of the last decade, George W. Bush. "It's my experience that people who have had issues with alcohol and are now clean and sober, they go through a transformation and they have come to the other end of a painful experience and they are usually wiser. I think a lot of people see George W. Bush as being a caricature, but in fact, this is a very, very complex individual who I think perhaps, we may never hear of it, but had some issues with all the power and the privilege he was given. I think it takes a lot of humility and I think I've seen that in George W. Bush to be able to be the person he is today. . . . and to deal with the pain of lots of failures and being considered a failure and not an intelligent person and being the butt of many jokes. I think in some ways, and it goes beyond his story, I think that the connection between George W. Bush and President Obama—these two Presidents—is that George W. Bush, fairly or unfairly, was seen of the butt of a lot of jokes and was disrespected in many, many ways by the public. President Obama has been disrespected in many, many ways because of his color so I think that's where the connection is. I think there is a fundamental and deep hurt that both men carry."

While that is certainly an interesting perspective, we need to be much further along than we currently are. We want an accounting for the wrongs heaped upon us and our ancestors, and we want America to accept responsibility for its part in our undoing. For race relations to improve, it's vital that everyone in our country recognize that Black folks have had their political voices strangled by a government system bent on silencing us. We want to know that America is willing to redress this travesty. The problems are far too great to ignore, and will, if not addressed, bring down our entire nation. A country that condones injustice, disregards the suffering of others, and looks the other way when its people are in need will perish.

We all need to identify the important issues and address them head on. Bishop Jakes thinks it's important to challenge ourselves: "One of the great problems we have in this country is that when we talk about bigotry, we see white sheets and burning crosses, hanging nooses on doors, and these types of vulgarities. That definition of racism or bigotry is so narrow that it gives us an easy pass to excuse ourselves if we do not have that type of blatant racism of our historical past. But the reality is all people fight against the tendency to have biases about a person based on externals—whether it be their clothing, their hair, the way they express themselves, their skin. And what we have to do becomes an issue of the heart. We have to begin to challenge ourselves to be our best selves."

Being discriminated against based merely on the color of our skin has created a separate society that amplifies disadvantage and the effects of poverty. In the Black community, there is a middle class, but in general, poverty and joblessness are the norm. Blacks are almost twice as likely to be unemployed as Whites. Schools in Black neighborhoods are grossly underfunded compared to White schools, and Black children don't get a quality education as a result. Economic opportunity is a misnomer for Blacks in many cases, and poverty is much more widespread. Economic downturns, like the recession that began in 2008, are felt much harder in Black communities with longer-term, calamitous effects.

Discrimination on the job and in education reduces employment opportunities and prevents Blacks from rising to the top. This, in turn, means they are underrepresented in politics and in Congress, and as we know from our history, taxation without representation is not the way our democracy works. Black representation in Congress in greater numbers means the Black community can have better access to the very power structures capable of bringing about change.

The legal system has dealt especially harsh blows to the Black community by codifying and enforcing unconstitutional laws that violate basic human rights. Our legal system has been notoriously prejudiced in the courts, and as a result, Blacks are denied equal justice under the law. Blacks are incarcerated in greater numbers than Whites, Blacks are disproportionately represented on death row, and Blacks are often given harsher sentences for similar crimes committed by Whites.

Few issues are as emotionally fraught or anxiety inducing as health issues, and in the Black community we see the long-term effects that racism has had when we look at people's physical and mental health. In many cases, Blacks suffer and die from preventable or treatable diseases caused by poverty and poor diet, which is directly tied to the lack of access to—and money to pay for—healthy, nutritional food. We see this in the high incidence of hypertension, heart disease, and diabetes in adults, but also in the epidemic of the onset of diabetes in Black children. Often, poverty, lack of access to medical care, and lack of education means more Blacks die from preventable or curable diseases than Whites do. The rate of HIV/AIDS infections in the Black community has reached alarming levels in the last decade, and according to the Center for Disease Control (CDC), Blacks are by far the ethnic group most affected by HIV/AIDS. In 2007, the CDC found that "[Blacks] accounted for almost half (46 percent) of people living with a diagnosis of HIV infection."

Shirley Sherrod, who was abruptly forced to tender her resignation as the Georgia State Director of Rural Development for the U.S. Department of Agriculture, said it best: "My message is that we've got to get beyond race. We have to get to a point where we can work with each other. That's why I tell the story of how I was transformed. When you look at everything that's happened to me and my family, and if I can then still help a White man and not look at the fact that he's White, or help a Hispanic person and not look at the fact that they're Hispanic—but that they're a human being, and someone who needs help—then I go and do that (help). That's where we all have to get to."

Finally, no matter what, it is important to recognize, as Bishop T. D. Jakes put it, "History handed African Americans a spoon, and the general population a shovel, and said, 'Dig your way up.' If we don't have the same tools, and the same resources, and the same opportunities, we can't get to the same destination as effectively. Many people think (of) various solutions to resolve that—from affirmative action to reparations. At the end of the day, whether we get a bigger shovel or not, we just have to put our spoons together and work harder to go forward—and forgiveness is a part of that process."

So as you can tell, I've been immersed in this topic for quite some time, and I've interviewed many powerful men and women on the subject. That's what propelled me to write this book in the first place. I felt that it was my responsibility to chronicle all that I have learned and experienced. It's my duty to share this information in the hope that maybe in some way it will help to bring about change.

Before we get too far down this path of finding a solution, I want to tell you about my first few days at the White House, what I saw, and how it became obvious to me that we have a long way to go to better understand, and hopefully rectify, this country's astounding racial inequality.

COVERING THE
WHITE HOUSE

Typically, 5:00 a.m. has always been that haunting hour, the ungodly time to get moving for the day. On January 13, 1997, the alarm startled me awake, and immediately thoughts of my imposing day swirled about me. I could see what I was faced with, as if a hologram of the day were before me. I just stood there frozen and watching. The stress was heavy; it would be my first day on the job. Despite the early hour, I received several phone calls from friends and family who felt every bit of the pressure, as they knew this was a big deal. I was carrying a part of them with me to the most recognized building in the world where history on every front has been made. The stakes were high. I appreciated the well wishes. I really needed them because my nerves were jumbled as I was embarking on a new adventure, an adventure that did not have a training manual or someone to guide me through the complicated maze of the politics at the White House.

I appreciated the surroundings of my parents' familiar kitchen. The noise of the early morning TV news played in the background to give me that needed distraction to make me feel more comfortable. I could not settle in too much, as the reports included a brief mention of a White House ceremony for some World War II vets scheduled for later that day.

My brother, Robert Jr., was there, and so was my dad. My mom made her normal small breakfast for us, and we ate in the dining room off of the L-shaped kitchen. In my excited state, I wolfed down my food, but I still needed more than just a stoking from a warm breakfast. I come from a strong religious background where faith was always an essential part of our lives. My family's belief in God has been a saving grace that has helped us deal with the struggles of being Black in America—the unavoidable ugliness that comes with racism—and helped us deal with the everyday knocks that happen to all people.

I knew that the reassurance I needed could come only from the Divine, and my daddy sensed my anticipation and anxiety. He wanted to begin the day in a conversation with God, so he gathered us together in a circle. We joined hands. He interceded on my behalf, and dutifully asked for God's guidance and blessings in this new chapter of my life.

Both of my parents come from modest, rural upbringings, and as we stood there together as a family, I could tell they were proud of me. Especially my father. At that moment he seemed to reach from his hometown of Sparks, Maryland, all the way to 1600 Pennsylvania Avenue. I'm sure that neither one of my parents ever imagined their daughter would be working at the epicenter of the most powerful nation in the world. But then, neither had I.

Except for a childhood visit as a tourist with my mother, I had never come close to the inner workings of the Executive Mansion. The only connection I'd ever had to the President of the United States was the picture of John F. Kennedy, which hung in my parents' home for as long as I could remember.

I grew up in a middle-class household where my dad was the major breadwinner, and he made my mother's dreams come true. She had a brand-new house that was nicely furnished, she was given fur coats, and my brother and I attended the university where my mother worked for over forty years. But that doesn't mean my parents didn't make sacrifices early on. If not for those sacrifices, I don't think this day would have been possible. My parents believed in giving their children the best things in life they could offer.

They did everything they could to move us ahead, and at the top of the list was getting a good education, which is why they took me out of public school in second grade and put me in Catholic school. It was during the really tough time of school busing in Baltimore, and my parents felt I would be safer at Catholic school. At the time, kids were bused from their all-Black neighborhood schools and put into predominantly White schools in a failed effort to integrate the schools and to improve the Black kids' education.

Icy January winds followed me southward that morning on my fifty-mile commute to Washington, D.C. I walked briskly through Lafayette Park along a red brick path strewn with lifeless, brown leaves that moved energetically on the frosty draft. The bronze statue of Andrew Jackson astride a horse rose majestically from the center of the park, watching over his place in history.

There it was. The White House. For a few moments, I stood nearly frozen. I was standing in front of the President's house, a place that hasn't always been favorable to African Americans or women, especially the slaves forced to erect it. I thought of those poor slaves, and the cruel irony of their laboring under the yoke of servitude to construct a house for the leader of a free, democratic nation.

Determined not to appear like a rookie, I composed myself, and set about gaining access to the White House complex. I waited in the bitter cold for at least ten minutes before finally getting cleared by security. And then I was in. After walking down the historic Northwest Driveway and entering the press briefing area, I saw a rush of activity.

Inside the commotion-filled space, reporters dashed about, but there seemed to be a semblance of order inside the melee. Camera crews, sound and lighting technicians, producers and reporters were chasing down the facts behind the story of the overlooked veterans—the story I had seen earlier on TV at my parents' house.

The podium with the famous Presidential Seal was there, and behind it was the familiar royal blue curtain that serves as a backdrop. That part looked like the Press Briefing Room I had seen countless times on television, but in seconds the illusion of grandeur and power portrayed on camera was destroyed. Nothing that I had ever seen on TV could have prepared me for the naked truth of what lay before me.

At first, I couldn't believe my eyes, so I looked again. I saw the rest of the room—the part that, thankfully, America doesn't see on camera. What isn't visible to viewers is a large, messy, fifty-by-twenty-foot room that looks like an old recycling bin! Newspapers were strewn all over the floor and jammed underneath the theatre-style seats. Large television cables and ladders were scattered all over the place, and it made the room feel more like an Olympic obstacle course than the room where the U.S. President or his spokesperson addresses the American people. The squalor was just unbelievable.

There were still more surprises to come. While the Briefing Room on the ground floor was startling, nothing could have prepared me for my "office." I made my way downstairs and headed for my booth, trying to take in everything that I was seeing along the way. It didn't take long before I got to a spot that looked like it was filled with a bunch of old telephone stalls, and it had several broken-down cubicles that had seen better days. I know from stories told by veteran reporters that it didn't always look this way.

Helen Thomas recalled that in 1961 the Briefing Room looked more like a spacious living room filled with sofas. She said, "They had a big sort of reception room where we all hung out. We could basically see people coming and going. But, maybe there were fifty people. There weren't even that many who were here all the time." Apparently, over the years, things in the Briefing Room changed as the public's interest in presidential news increased.

Some of this interest was due to John F. Kennedy's time in office. He and First Lady Jacqueline Kennedy made the White House and life in the East Wing seem glamorous. The public's fascination with the White House mushroomed. This, in turn, meant more TV coverage, more reporters, more radio, and lots more equipment. It was inevitable that the media would outgrow their quarters. So much so that some of the plaster-of-Paris walls were literally crumbling, and what looked like metal wiring holding the plaster was exposed.

When shown to my booth, I almost laughed out loud. It was so pathetic and forlorn that it seemed as if someone had played a cruel joke on me. Maybe I was being hazed on my first day! It looked like nothing more than a narrow, dirty, old phone booth—and was about that width. In it was a large reel-to-reel machine, an audio mixer, and a telephone. The application for this job should have contained a warning: claustrophobics need not apply! The room was about six feet deep and looked as if it hadn't been cleaned or painted in thirty years. The ceiling was made of what looked like hazardous asbestos tiles, but the walls were my favorite part. They were covered in yellowing, coffee-stained paper. The overall effect was midcentury dingy, not exactly glamorous or prestigious, as I had imaged at breakfast just a few hours ago. And yes, rodents came down to our cramped area, too. And later I found out that if it rained, there was the threat of basement flooding. For the record, White House officials have told us we are not their tenants, but it is a General Services Administration (GSA) issue.

Not knowing what else to do, I placed my bags inside the tiny room, or at least I tried to. The only problem was that my pocketbook and briefcase were too large for the little stall. I took a deep breath and was determined not to let frustration or discontent take over. Any illusions of grandeur that I might have had were quickly dashed by the reality of my microscopic office.

I came to realize that the antagonistic relationship between the White House and reporters meant that White House officials really couldn't care less how reporters live for eight or more hours of the day. The White House's neglect of the reporters' workspace certainly contributes to the polite but adversarial relationship. What else could explain the horrible conditions of our meager offices?

Unlike most others, White House reporters rarely have direct access to the person they are covering. Reporters get frustrated when they don't have the ability to question the key players in their stories, and they hate relying on staffers all the time. And when you cover national news, there isn't anyone more important than the U.S. President. On Capitol Hill, for example, you can pick up the phone and get a U.S. Senator or Member of Congress to talk to you directly. But that's just not so at the White House. A Clinton Administration official suggested that it's this lack of one-on-one contact with the President that makes the White House Press Corps so "hyperaggressive" as a group. What's odd, though, is that no one in the Press Corps ever seems to take their meager accommodations personally. They work in really cramped quarters right on top of each other, and they take it in stride. It's all part of the territory. You sacrifice comfort for proximity because that's just the way it is.

Nevertheless, reporters aren't the only ones fighting for access to the President. There are also plenty of officials at the White House who work for the Chief Executive and yet have little or no contact with him. Some of them have had their own rude awakenings once on the job. The first shocker is usually their accommodations, which almost always fall short of their expectations. Most just grin and bear it as part of the price they pay for being in the West Wing. Even former Secretary of State Colin Powell had to adjust some of his unrealistic expectations.

At one time, there were pundits who considered Powell the only man of color able to mount a viable campaign for the Oval Office, so hearing him describe his modest office was a reality check. When he first arrived at the West Wing, his quarters were more fitting for an army private than a battle-decorated general. "If you're not the National Security Advisor, the President, or the Vice President, or the Chief of Staff, you are living and trying to work out of a closet. And I think people think everyone there has a beautiful view of Pennsylvania Avenue and the North Lawn, and Lafayette Park, but that is not always the case," said Powell.

When Colin Powell was Deputy National Security Advisor, his White House space was so small and insignificant it was almost nonexistent. As Powell recalled, "I came in as National Security Advisor from being a Corps Commander in Germany where I had a huge headquarters and a huge office. I found myself tucked in an office the size of a closet wondering what fate had done to stick me inside this tiny little cubbyhole." The cubbyhole Powell referred to was just a few steps from the spacious office of his immediate boss, the National Security Advisor. Looking back now, Powell is able to laugh about his cramped White House quarters, but it wasn't so funny back then. As he said, "My first day there, January 2nd or 3rd, 1987, I'm sitting in this closet trying to figure out: Now what are we going to do?"

A visit by Vice President George H. W. Bush quelled any concerns he had, though. Powell smiled when he recalled the incident, and he still finds it funny. Powell, who attempted to recreate the noise he heard that day, said, "Suddenly, there was this explosion of noise in the outer office." Mimicking Bush, Powell then exclaimed, "'Where is he? Where is he? Is he here yet? Is he here yet?' Suddenly, George H. W. Bush, the Vice President of the United States, appears in this little closet. And there I am, until two days earlier, a very, very, very subordinate Lieutenant General Corps Commander, and here I am with the Vice President of the United States visiting me in my office which is the size of a cubbyhole."

He remained in the tight quarters for nine months until he was appointed National Security Council Advisor. While the promotion may have brought a much bigger office, there was one tiny drawback, or so he thought at first—Powell had to share a tiny bathroom the size of a walk-in closet with Vice President Bush. This spare space came equipped with the barest of essentials, and included a sink and toilet. But as luck would have it, it was this very lack of space, and Powell's constant contact with Vice President Bush, that was the beginning of their long friendship.

As Powell said, "That is where we developed a friendship, sharing a bathroom. And then he made me Chairman of the Joint Chiefs of Staff a little while later." As it turned out, this fortuitous shortage of bathrooms and office space created other potential opportunities for bonding with other White House aides and officials. Bush and Powell weren't the only ones with access to this exclusive restroom; it was also designated for use by the Chief of Staff and other workers in that part of the West Wing.

My first day not only cramped my space but my style, as well. I stumbled, literally and figuratively, into everything. Truthfully, the whole experience was awkward and ungainly, and left me unnerved for months. I always felt as if I was physically off balance. To their credit, my colleagues were professional, even polite, but most everyone was too busy to offer me any kind of assistance.

It was seven days before the January 20, 1997, Presidential Inauguration of William Jefferson Clinton. The Clinton White House was entering its second term after defeating Senator Bob Dole's Republican bid for President, and the administration was in the midst of battling the Paula Jones scandal.

With the Paula Jones thing hanging over their heads and dominating the news cycle, the Clinton Administration wisely knew that they needed a "feel good" event that touched his base. So they decided it was time to rewrite the book on the egregious omission of Black soldiers in the bestowing of military honors.

The correction was made by belatedly presenting the Medal of Honor to seven men who had come to represent the shameful treatment of all Black soldiers during World War II. These men had valiantly fought for freedoms that they had been denied in their own country. Along with dozens of other reporters, I was escorted to the East Room on the State Floor of the Residence to witness this historic moment.

On the State Floor are some of the rooms you get to see on the public tour of the White House, such as the Red Room, the Blue Room, the Green Room, the State Dining Room, and the East Room. The White House is as much a museum as it is a functional space for a range of activities, as well as the living quarters for the First Family. The East Room is a large, elegant, multipurpose room that is sparsely furnished with eighteenth- and nineteenth-century antiques and paintings (including one of Gilbert Stuart's full-length portraits of George Washington). The magnitude of the White House ceremony matched the grandeur of the East Room's oversized curtains, paintings, and massive chandeliers.

Traditionally, Presidents have used the room for large gatherings such as dances, concerts, weddings, funerals, and bill-signing ceremonies. This room has witnessed the spectrum of American history, but on this day, it was being used for a ceremony that would attempt to right a wrong willfully committed by the U.S. Military and Government. The room was awash with the gentle sounds of stringed instruments used to set the tone for the ceremony. When we got there, it was standing room only, and the overflow was made up of at least one hundred journalists and numerous guests—most of whom were African American.

I was about to cover my first major story for American Urban Radio Networks, and it was a happy coincidence that it perfectly suited my audience. In the broadcasting world, *urban* is often a euphemism for Black listeners, or even more pejorative for mainstream news, a diminishing term like *minority*. This story was at once Black history and Black news. Personally, I felt that this was just one more reminder that despite delays, justice can sometimes prevail even at the highest levels of power. By taking the lead on this, President Clinton was indicating that he had put the welcome mat out for Blacks at the White House. It seemed like a symbolic gesture of respect, and an unspoken promise that African Americans could move to positions of prominence in government and the White House.

As the ceremony got underway, I frantically took notes so that I could capture the moment for my listeners. I knew that they would find this an important, historic moment, and here is what my notes say about the ceremony:

President Clinton opened by saying, "Today we recognize seven men as being among the bravest of the brave. When victory was complete in World War II, our government made a pledge to correct cases in which Medals of Honor were deserved but not awarded. Today, America honors that pledge. On behalf of the United States Congress I award the Medal of Honor, our nation's highest military award, to Vernon Baker."

The presentation of the awards was the result of a Shaw University study commissioned by the Pentagon to probe disparities in the selection process for the Medals of Honor. Out of the 432 presented the honor for service in World War II, not even one serviceman of the more than one million Blacks who had served were given the Medal of Honor. Half a century earlier, President Harry Truman honored twenty-eight overlooked veterans of the war with the Medal of Honor, but still not one Black soldier was given a medal. The Medal of Honor is revered in the military because of the heroic, selfless sacrifice involved. It is only awarded when soldiers go "above and beyond the call of duty" without any consideration for their own safety. It's especially shameful that countless Black soldiers were denied this kind of recognition for their sacrifices when countless examples existed.

It must have been unbearable and defeating to wait year after year for some sort of justice, especially in the face of such iniquity. Those of us attending heard President Clinton say, "History is being made whole." Clinton noted that other Blacks who deserved the same honor had also served without reward. Clinton said, "Today we fill in the gap of that picture and give a group of heroes who also loved peace, but adapted themselves to war . . . the tribute that has always been their due."

The conferring of medals that day was the largest ever for Black veterans. Only one of the award recipients would be present, and five of the honorees were given the distinction posthumously. Their bravery under fire had been overlooked for far too long, and it was gratifying to see this survivor finally receive his medal, along with the thanks of his President. The sole recipient to stand before the President was seventy-seven-year-old Vernon Baker, who was visibly choked up as his Commander in Chief placed the Medal of Honor around his neck. It was emotional for all of us to see the tears that flowed down Vernon Baker's caramel cheeks.

Then we learned Vernon Baker's story, and I was personally overcome with sadness, anger, and shame at the way our country had treated him. On April 5, 1945, Vernon Baker was a kid of twenty-two. He fought in Northern Italy, where he bravely led his all-Black platoon behind enemy lines, despite having his troops riddled with gunfire. They were able to cut enemy communication lines, but they needed reinforcements if their mission was to succeed without heavy casualties. Baker's White commander knew this and left, promising to return with more troops. Instead, this commander never returned with the reinforcements, and he left his own men to die. That commander's actions can only be considered a war crime, and it is an abhorrent embarrassment to the military and the United States.

Later, Baker found out that his platoon had killed twenty-six Germans, but of the twenty-six men he'd arrived with, only eight survived. Military records showed that, contrary to what the military brass said at the time, Baker's bravery was nominated for a Congressional Medal of Honor. It seems that the necessary paperwork somehow "mysteriously" never materialized. Instead, Baker was awarded the Distinguished Service Cross, the nation's second highest honor.

While there certainly wasn't any shame in receiving this medal, it wasn't what he deserved—which is why in 1994 Baker decided it was time to find out what had happened to his Medal of Honor. His quest led him to uncover declassified accounts of that day's battle. From those accounts, he learned that his company commander, the one who'd left his own troops to die, had reported that the other Black soldiers had been cowards, and were too afraid to fight. This commander had lied to his superiors and told them the Black soldiers had no stomach for combat.

We were all grateful that after decades of racially imposed obscurity, these men were finally receiving their due. The other heroes who received medals that day were Edward Carter Jr., John R. Fox, Will F. James Jr., Ruben Rivers, Charles L. Thomas, and George Watson. It strains belief that their amazing deeds were never recognized or heralded before this. For example, Edward Carter was shot five times while crossing an open field to aid a platoon leader. Even with mortal wounds, he continued to advance, running into eight enemy soldiers. He killed six of them and brought two back for interrogation.

Shamefully, this American's extreme bravery under fire was never awarded, and he died thinking that his country didn't value his courage. I would come to learn that this kind of recognition for people of color was indeed rare, and such oversights were common. The federal quadrant that includes the White House, Capitol Hill, and the Pentagon is known as a White male "fraternity" that supports itself.

Finally, the time had come for these men, and the truth about their bravery under fire was rescued from obscurity and made a part of our official history. At the end of the ceremony, a fervent chorus of "amen" resounded throughout the East Room, and it transformed decades of deep sadness into heartfelt praise. The contributions of these men were no longer just the memories for their families.

In the end, America finally said, "Thank you," and showed its gratitude, albeit fifty years later. I felt blessed to share the news of the correction with my audience, because I knew it wouldn't be a top news story on the major networks. For them, it would fall into the "in other news" category. Sharing these stories with my listeners was important, because as African Americans, we all feel a bit of recognition is due as history books often do not tell our story, or even if they do, it's almost always conveniently riddled with inaccuracies.

After witnessing this special moment, I have to admit that I felt a little better about my first day. But it was still obvious I was a greenhorn, and not all of the members of the Press Corps had warmed up to me. There was more to my initiation than just being the new kid on the block. Many of the reporters were at first indifferent toward me, but I chalked a lot of it up to the competitive nature of most White House journalists, and journalists in general. We're all trying to get a jump on the next big story, so competition is part of the job description.

It still seemed as if there was more to the cold shoulder than just competitiveness. I had replaced Bob Ellison, a man who had been a close friend to many of the reporters, and he had been highly respected. These guys had spent countless days and nights together in the subterranean newsroom, and as the new kid, I was a constant reminder that their old friend was gone. At first they weren't willing to tell me about even basic information like the daily routine.

At some point, I got a lucky break and happened to overhear talk about something called "the gaggle." Two days went by before I finally mustered up the courage to follow the rest of the Press Corps upstairs for the gaggle in the Press Secretary's office. As I found out, this was the morning meeting held daily by then-Presidential Spokesman Mike McCurry to discuss the President's schedule for the day. It was also a time for the spokesman to be advised of the questions reporters wanted answered by him, or preferably, the President.

The brief meeting reminded me of a football huddle where the coach stands in the middle of the team strategizing the play of the day. During the gaggle, national or international news items surface and are essential to us getting good stories for networks and papers. Some examples have included the scandal that involved presidential campaign donors staying in the Lincoln Bedroom in exchange for their contributions, air strikes against Iraq, the First Family's holiday dinner menu, and even the first dog getting neutered.

At first, being unaware of all the unwritten rules made my job nightmarish, and in defense, I kept my booth door closed. What I didn't realize at the time was, by keeping my door shut, I missed important intercom announcements and the two-minute warning issued by the Press Secretary right before each briefing. The daily struggle of playing catch-up and trying to figure out how things worked was making me a basket case. I was starting to feel as if I were banging my head on walls that were slowly closing in on me more each day.

I was really beginning to hate the job, and I was on the verge of walking away. I didn't tell anyone, except my mother. She listened to my concerns and gave me some good advice. She told me that if I resigned after being there for such a short time, people wouldn't think I had quit. They would assume I'd been fired. She suggested I put in two years, no matter what. My mother was right, at least a two-year commitment was required. It was time to get to work. She's since gone on to her reward, and about two decades later, I still treasure her confidence in me.

And I'm still here.

SPECIALTY MEDIA

President George W. Bush once said before an interview in the flying Oval Office on our way to view New Orleans that he wished there were more minorities in the White House Briefing Room. I join him in that thought. The problem is serious when you have only a small group of people who herd and flow together. Often times, issues of race are not on the agenda of questioning at all. A lot of times the only voice asking the questions that are not always "above the fold" are White journalists who are asking questions for the most part that do not target segmented groups in this country. That's where specialty media comes into play. We are the ones behind that invisible line of the first two rows in the White House Briefing Room.

Unfortunately, the "specialty media" label puts us at an automatic disadvantage as we are immediately relegated to second-class White House media status. It is a huge deal because I am literally right behind the mainstream, and I watch as they get more attention with their questions, which are not ones that are typically of concern to minorities. We are the group that does not always travel with the President in the Washington, D.C. limits or around the United States, and forget traveling out of the country. It's extremely rare and is often attributed to budgetary restrictions.

But often when the numbers are tabulated, the ratings of the specialty media audience rival that of some of the "mainstream media." You might be wondering who is considered specialty media by the White House. We are the organizations—American Urban Radio Networks, Univision, BET, *Essence*, *Ebony*, LGBT outlets—media that is not predominately viewed, listened to, or read by a majority of the population.

We are the group that does not always make it into those big meetings. They are reserved for the major networks and cable channels, large city newspapers, and corporate radio. This is an unfortunate practice that is exercised by the White House and the inner circles of the White House Press Corps. This labeling seems like a throwback to a time when classism was much more accepted. The sad truth is that it happened back then and is still happening. It's an odd and unmistakable representation of the society at large in which the minority voices have less of an opportunity to share their views. It's our daily struggle to ensure that we are heard.

Make no mistake, being a White House Correspondent is a badge of honor, but in many cases there are odds that are institutional, uncalled for, and simply hard to change. As I quickly learned during my on-the-job training in the Press Corps, being a minority among this group means being automatically pigeon-holed. For the most part, minorities are judged whether we are in specialty media or part of a team in a mainstream news operation. The proof is in the well-documented history of the positive and negative aspects of life inside that White House Briefing Room.

The pioneer of the White House Black reporters covering this prestigious beat is St. Louis native Harry S. McAlpin. In 1944, he was the first African American journalist to be granted access to a White House press conference. He was a small-framed man who worked for, at that time, what was called the Negro press. He also covered the White House for *The Chicago Defender*, and his reports were often distributed to other Black newspapers around the country. He paved the way by working in the White House and reporting on the actions of the President of the United States, despite protests from others. McAlpin, a persistent reporter and gifted wordsmith, was confronted with constant taunts and warnings from other reporters who felt threatened and protective of their formerly all-White group. Now, some seventy years later, while it is less overt, some of those attitudes are prevalent to this day.

McAlpin's story was like that of most any other budding journalist. He always strived to obtain direct access to the principle he was charged with reporting on. He was dedicated to getting the story firsthand, not content with just accepting prepared statements. So when he went to his first White House press conference, he was confronted. A White reporter told him it would be easier if he just waited outside. He would be provided with all of the necessary notes and would have the same information as everyone else if he just waited on the other side of the door. Undeterred, McAlpin attended the press conference and even made a point of approaching President Roosevelt for good measure.

During a 1950s appearance on Edward R. Murrow's *This I Believe* radio show, McAlpin (forty-six at the time) said he was "not responsible" but "proud" of being born a Negro. It took a sitting President to right the deliberate wrong that was an unfortunate result of persistent racism. The thirty-second U.S. President welcomed the Black journalist into that historic press conference, but the issues of discrimination did not stop there for him. McAlpin still felt the brunt of discrimination and was told that if he stepped on any reporters' toes there would be a riot.

My appearance in the Briefing Room was a red flag for some folks. I remember when I asked the late journalism veteran Helen Thomas for an interview the first time and she said no as she did not want to be considered a Lebanese American. I did not understand fully why she said that. But I got it. Because of my push for news on Black America, people in that room immediately thought I was a militant. Actually, I am just the opposite. Initially I saw myself as more of a conduit, a way to funnel information to those who were not being adequately served by the mainstream press. But I soon began to realize that I had to take a bit more of an aggressive role. If I thought certain issues needed to be addressed, I couldn't afford to sit back and wait for the answers because they would never come. I needed to make sure that issues affecting all Americans were being addressed. Helen also told me that she did not want to be classified by race. I did not understand where that came from. She said she was an American. Well, I had some late-breaking news for her and everyone else. I am an American, too, and I'm the face of the part of American that is often ignored, and that needs to change.

According to Dr. Martha Joynt Kumar, Political Science Professor at Towson University, I scored more one-on-one radio interviews with President Clinton than any other reporter. As you can imagine, the other journalists were not happy with that outcome, so much so that they even circulated a petition demanding equal access. Of course, that enviable access didn't come by accident. I worked hard to get noticed and to establish my place among my competitive colleagues. At first I sat in the very back of the room, actually in the end seat on the sixth of seven rows. I never liked my seat and would always move up to the rows closer to the podium when others would leave their seat.

I quickly found out that was not only frowned upon but aggressively discouraged. Each of the seats is labeled for the designated reporter. Mine read "Sheridan Broadcasting." The company I work for is a made up of several entities. That is why it is called American Urban Radio Networks (AURN). At that time I was not a member of the pool, a smaller subset of reporters who travel with the President when he is in smaller and tight venues. I was told by the then-President of the White House Correspondents' Association that I could have that seat if I joined the pool. Well, I immediately replied that it already was my seat, since Sheridan and AURN are one and the same. The president of the association and the other complaining reporter countered by saying that I had misunderstood what was said. No, I fully understood that they were trying to exert authority over me, as if they controlled my location and thus I should be grateful. It was a situation that closely mirrored McAlpin's experiences decades ago.

However, I did learn quickly that when an administration wants access to a specific community—Blacks, Hispanics, Asians, LGBT groups—suddenly the specialty media is in big demand. Then, we are no longer the minority questioning voice relegated to the balcony seats. We are given front-row access and first-class treatment. It's a precarious position to be in because our ultimate responsibility is to our audience. The reason why I am there is to provide a voice of questioning that may not otherwise be there. I have found out that if it's advantageous for an administration to seek out our community, I am going to make sure that some of our pressing issues are given attention. It has to be a give-and-take situation.

Working in "specialty media" is certainly no guarantee of a stellar career in journalism or an avenue for exclusive interviews with the President or the First Family, but from time to time it can help. Like any leader, the President is of two minds when it comes to the power of the press. There are times he may deftly and skillfully use the media to get his agenda before the American people, and at other times he may detest them for their ability to create political mayhem by probing beyond the prepared statements.

President Clinton's Press Secretary, Mike McCurry, calls this an "amicable adversarial relationship." He said, "There is no substitute for the role the press plays, even in the days of the Internet and social media networks. But there is also no substitute for staff people at the White House who serve as 'advocates' for the press even if they cannot always deliver. The relationship is symbiotic, and when it becomes polarized and poisoned, nothing good happens. I think that's where we are too often these days—too much 'adversarialism' and cynicism, and not enough discussion of the things both sides of the relationship have in common."

I can certainly attest to the fact that any time the White House staff begins to display arrogance by insinuating that they have the media under control, or they assume they can successfully manipulate the Press Corps and tightly manage the news, it invariably backfires with unpleasant, unintentional consequences.

Those of us in specialty media know how much Presidents like to manage the news and try to use it to their advantage whenever they can. We know that there are times when our access to a particular voting bloc, demographic, or audience is beneficial. Whenever the White House wants to get their message to any of these groups, they come to us knowing that while we may not be the largest media outlets, we have the ability to reach niche audiences. We haven't always been front and center in the Briefing Room, but from time to time, our access to special audiences and our unique demographic expertise makes us invaluable.

While interviewing Mike McCurry for this book, he admitted that specialty media were not the first media that they went to at the White House. He told me that certain news organizations got the Press Secretary and President's attention and were a priority.

"Yes, there is a news hierarchy at the White House. If you want to be at the top of a 'preferred' list valued by the President and Senior Administration Officials," McCurry said, "work for a large circulation news organization that has a bigger impact on public opinion and public attitudes. Media in Washington is dominated by the networks, the large newspapers, and the big wire services—in essence, the media outlets that have the maximum impact on the information culture in Washington."

Obviously, those reporters get to go to the head of the line during Q&A, but with persistence, it is possible to get noticed. I wasn't so lucky at first, but I have managed to carve a place for myself in the pecking order, despite the fact that my news organization isn't mainstream. I have always been proud of being a reporter for specialty media, but I have always tried to elbow my way closer to the front of the room. Early on I once asked the "President's Mouthpiece" if this was fair. In typical McCurry fashion, he pondered my question for a second, took a breath, and then slowly answered, "Yeah, it's not only fair; it's necessary. You are trying to get your information to the widest number of Americans in the shortest amount of time possible."

Marlin Fitzwater, the White House Press Secretary for Presidents Ronald Reagan and George H. Bush, reiterated McCurry's sentiments, saying, "Generally speaking, [we] go with the biggest organizations first that reach the most people. That is why Presidents always call on AP, UPI, and wire services first, because they service everybody. The theory being that if you are specialty media and you don't get a chance to ask your question, at least the wire services are there to ask it for you. But this is almost always dictated by the size of the audience."

But when it comes to those news organizations that are not mainstream media, Tony Fratto, Deputy White House Press Secretary of the George W. Bush Administration, said, "We are very proud of the way we meld together in terms of our outlook in the way we think. But we still have communities in a way, and

I think some of those communities like and still have a need for their own unique selection of topics."

This theory doesn't work for me, though. I report on everything at the White House, and my focus is on urban and minority America. The wires simply don't ask the kinds of questions I do unless there's a strong White House push on the issues that affect my listeners. When Fitzwater gave me a breakdown of the access pyramid for the White House Press Corps, he explained that my type of reporting was at the bottom of the pyramid. "The television networks represent the next largest mass audience in the country. Then you go to the largest newspapers and magazines. So you kind of work your way down the food chain."

In his ten years as Press Secretary, Fitzwater says he wanted to give as much access to the President as he could. He said his position was, "All media have a right to access to the President, whether it's a newsletter for a company, a radio station representing minority groups or ethnic interests, or a mainstream newspaper in foreign countries. They all have a right to know what the government is doing and that the White House needs to come up with some method for responding to those needs. Specialty media in a White House context usually means that they have a certain group of people who make sure that those media receive information. I think that is valuable and every White House has to do that." Maybe some of this is slowly changing in the "new media" era.

Mike McCurry noted, "In the past, there were niche audiences with very special needs. But now, every audience is a niche or targeted market. I think the key word now is 'fragmented.' There is no national, cohesive audience except in very rare circumstances. Every audience has specialty publications, blogs, or newsletters that require different kinds of responses from public information officers."

While it makes sense for the White House to see us as "go to" people on issues that are important to our audiences, sometimes fate steps in and specialty media get a chance to be front and center because we have somehow caught the attention of the President or Press Secretary. One way to get the President's attention is to earn the respect of the President, First Lady, and the people in both press offices. The White House is a small, tight-knit group, and people on the inside talk to each other. So it's natural for them to notice when the President or First Lady likes someone. This can lead to more opportunities for one-on-one interviews, get you called on at briefings, and help you earn the trust and respect of key White House staff so that you have more chances for exclusive access. Broadcaster Tavis Smiley touched on the respect issue when he told me, "Even when you are a reporter, and you are sitting in front of the President, there is a certain level of deference in talking to the President. You don't want to be strident in your questions. You are trying to walk a tightrope in terms of getting him to open up and to say something, and at the same time, be respectful."

I know because I have benefited from this kind of attention. A good reporter can catch the attention of the President by being in the right place at the right time, and this kind of easy familiarity can be cultivated over time. If you don't sit in the first two rows, the chances of a specialty media reporter getting called on during a press conference rises exponentially if the President knows the reporter's name. One way to get to know the President is by taking every opportunity to familiarize him with you and your organization. Persistence and patience are key, and they do eventually pay off. And in a town where the currency is access to power, you can't ever give up. You would be amazed at how many doors are magically opened to you if the President knows you well enough to call you by name. There is no substitute for this kind of personal recognition. Luckily, I had learned this even before I got my job at the White House. I owe this important bit of intel to my cousin, former New York Congressman Edolphus Towns. He taught me that presidential recognition is just as important for the President as it is for the reporter, and this bit of advice has proven helpful to me in my career.

He once told me, "When people are called by name, it shows voters, 'Look, I am so concerned about you and what you have to say, that I even know your name. I want to listen to you. I want to hear you out.' And the fact that he has that ability to do it, it sort of helps him in terms of people feeling very comfortable with him. Also, that they feel that based on that, he is very sincere in whatever he is doing. So, I think it helps him in terms of his ability to govern because he's saying, 'Look, I know your name, I want to hear from you; what you are saying to me is very, very important. So go ahead and say it.'" Knowing this made me determined to find a way to get the President's attention. I knew what I had to do if I wanted to make a difference at my job, and thankfully, it didn't take long for me to get my chance.

It was a day like any other at the White House. I was standing on a lower step at the entrance to the press office. Just by chance, President Clinton walked through the corridor outside of that office. Seeing a few of us standing there, he popped his head through the doorway, came over to speak to us, and made chitchat with the staffers and interns. Not realizing I was a reporter, he was open, relaxed, and congenial. All I could think about was, "Girl, this is your chance, say something!" I put my hand out to shake his, and said, "Hello, my name is April Ryan, I'm the new White House Correspondent for American Urban Radio Networks."

The minute he heard the word *correspondent*, he turned on his heels and started to leave. I asked him to come back, which he politely did, and I asked,

"Would you please call on me at your next press conference?" Surprisingly, he agreed, and then walked off in the direction of the residence. I waited to see if he would call on me at the press conference the following week or if he had just been pacifying me, and when he didn't, I assumed that he had forgotten. I remember thinking at the time, "Why should he remember me? I'm just one of thousands of people he meets every week."

Another press conference followed soon after, and it gave me an opportunity to see for myself that the myths of his steel-trap memory definitely *aren't* exaggerated. He finally acknowledged me, allowing me to ask my question in front of everyone. Whether or not he called on me that day as a means of avoiding someone else's more difficult questions doesn't matter. I know that he called on me because he recognized me from before, and that kind of connection is difficult to come by in Washington. I realized I had something unique. This kind of access is vital for anyone working inside the Beltway. It doesn't matter if you're a senator, reporter, or lobbyist, if you don't have the kind of influence that gets your calls returned or your questions answered, you won't ever be at the top of the heap.

I can't do my job effectively without this kind of access and recognition from the President, and it has helped me get important one-on-one interviews with key players at the Executive Mansion, such as then First Ladies Hillary Rodham Clinton and Laura Bush, Presidents Clinton, George W. Bush, and Barack Obama, as well as many others. This kind of rapport is not a trivial thing, and is, in fact, one of the most important aspects of my job. Do I think that in some cases I got an interview because someone wanted to curry the favor of my audience? Or that they gave me an interview to distract Americans from the real issues of the day? Sure, but it's my job to get them to speak to me, whatever their real motivations may be, and I appreciate every opportunity.

Specialty media gets a real boost when the President calls on one of its reporters, even if the President or Press Secretary is calling on them to avoid questions from the big boys at the top of the pyramid. At times like these, we may be "used" to deflect or distract attention away from a controversial issue or scandal, but a smart reporter knows that this is also a chance to get valuable face time and national exposure for your company and your issues. This is a rare chance to stand out from the crowd. That's why one of the cardinal rules of being a White House reporter is that you *never* miss an opportunity to ask the President a question, ever.

You just have to know what motivates the White House to share or withhold information, and how to use this to your own ends. Every administration is naturally suspicious of the press, and it only reluctantly relinquishes information to the media; neither side trusts the other, and their motives are often at odds. As a result, building a relationship and instilling trust takes time and effort. Until a reporter earns the respect of White House staff, you are ignored and overlooked, never a good position for a reporter to be in.

I learned this quickly, so I never miss an opportunity to remind the White House of who I am and whom I work for. Spontaneous meetings like the one with President Clinton had big payoffs for me. The first time came when President Clinton selected me at a press conference on March 10, 1997. At the time, Clinton and Egyptian President Hosni Mubarak were holding a joint press conference at the White House, and Clinton was being bombarded with difficult questions about the Middle East peace process. Both Presidents took turns answering questions from both American and Egyptian reporters, and close to the end of the conference, President Clinton scanned the crowd and found me. At the time I remember wondering if he was calling on me because he wanted to put an end to the line of difficult questions about Middle East peace, but I didn't care. This was my chance to ask *my* question.

President Clinton pointed to me, and I gave him the unintentional reprieve he was looking for by asking a question related to Black civil rights and his stance on hiring welfare recipients at the White House. It was during the administration's welfare reform initiative, and I was anxious to hear how the White House would deal with the issue of getting welfare recipients off the dole and into the workplace—especially since many of the people being denied benefits were Black. What I hadn't anticipated was how that one question would immediately deflate the momentum of the previous line of questions. You could feel the energy in the room drop.

By breaking into the line of questions the big, front-row reporters had been working on, I effectively ended their temporary monopoly of the subject at hand. The other reporters surely were not happy, but I had my job to do, and I succeeded in getting the issue that my audience cared about in front of the President. White House reporters are notorious about complaining when someone breaks a roll in a line of questions—unless they're the ones doing the breaking, of course. They act as if it's an unspeakable crime, and look down their noses at you as if you were media slime. The big-shot reporters can get downright petulant about losing a turn, but only when it affects them directly.

To the hot shots in the front row, I had not only become media slime, I was an embarrassment. As far as I was concerned, what they thought didn't matter. I cared about what my audience thought—not the mainstream media. They never talked about my audience's issues. I had done my job as a competent reporter and gotten myself noticed by the President. The end result was that he got himself out of a tight situation, and my audience got to hear what he planned to do about the welfare issue and its impact on the Black community. After all was said and done, at least six welfare recipients were hired at the White House, and according to administration officials, only one of those hired resigned (for personal reasons).

After that news conference, the reporters returned to the press area, and I overheard some of the front-row reporters asking each other, "How did she get to ask a question? She has only been here for a few months. Who is she? Where did she come from?" I was the oddball because no one knew who I was, and I was from one of the lesser-known media outlets. That press conference got a lot of people thinking about AURN and about me, and it helped get a bunch of balls rolling in my career at the White House. Granted, the President hadn't called on me by name, but he did call on me. That was the start, and whatever it takes is the name of the game in this town.

I made a point of sending a thank you note to the President after that conference, and I was surprised when I received a kind reply in return . . . and grateful. His note was a sign that I was becoming a known commodity in the political structure at the White House. I was hopeful that this would lead to more regular opportunities to ask questions at press briefings, chances for face-to-face interviews, and possibly more. Coincidentally, not much later, I got a chance to interview the First Lady in an exclusive. It went so well, many of the staff talked about it afterward. In hindsight, it was most likely the President's favorable impression that helped open the door to my interview, but the fact that it went so well was all due to her. She was a warm, engaging, open, and intelligent interviewee, and her charm put me at ease and made things flow smoothly. I think she had a good time, too, because there was quite a bit of banter between the two of us, and she laughed often during the interview.

That interaction went so well that it got the attention of other press office staffers; later I heard that even the President mentioned how much Mrs. Clinton had enjoyed our time together. After that, one thing led to another, and soon my calls and requests were met with a more favorable response. In fact, I am almost certain that it was Mrs. Clinton's mention of the interview that reminded her husband of who I was and kept me on his radar screen, which, as it turns out, worked in my favor. It also didn't hurt my efforts to get as close as a reporter could with Mike McCurry, either.

At these briefings, Presidents will generally only be familiar with the names of a few select reporters, so they point to someone if they don't know their name but want to call on them. The real cache is when the President calls you by your first name. Anyone who has ever dealt with the White House knows this all too well.

You see this happen all the time. Unfortunately, in Washington, it's often *who* you know that matters, not *what* you know. Or in this case, who knows you or knows your name. There have been occasions when I have wondered, "Have I gotten where I am because of who I know or is it because of what I know? Or is it neither? Have I moved ahead, gotten recognized, been called on at a press conference, or gotten an interview because I knew somebody, or because I did a good job?" I guess the bigger question is, "Does it really matter?" If my audience gets to hear about the issues they care about from the leader of the free world and my bosses are happy, what difference does it make in the long run? Does it really matter if I got a chance to ask a question because the President wanted to dodge an uncomfortable line of questioning? Ultimately, I think the answer is "no." I'm here to ask questions and get the story; that's my job. I may have to work harder than the big, mainstream media outlets because I'm specialty media, but I still get my stories.

Sometimes the White House is focused on managing the news and controlling what's reported out there, and the President and his staff lose sight of how to get the media to work with them. That happens frequently, but while the White House may want a particular story or issue covered, we have an agenda, too, and it's not always to ambush the President. We need good stories, and coming up with ideas, leads, sources, and background information can be a bear to find or get access to. That's why we are always bugging the principals and insiders for tips.

You would think that they would realize this and feed us useful, timely, or exclusive information. Unfortunately, what we often get instead is misleading, incomplete, or inconsequential leads. They are just giving us what they want us to hear, not what we need to know—which is too bad. The American people have a right to know how their leader is governing, so it would make things easier for everyone if staffers would just cooperate. They know that the minute we sniff out a cover up or reluctance to share information, we will be like bird dogs on point.

We will dig, pester, and question until we get the answers we feel we are owed, and the White House could save everyone the rancor and mistrust if they would be more forthcoming. I guess it's just too hard for the politicians and strategists to let go of control. Information is power in Washington, and controlling it is viewed as paramount by the government. Maybe this is why some attempts by the White House to reach out to the media backfire, especially when trying to reach specialty media. You can't have it both ways: either you are going to be open with reporters and share news or not, but you can't control every bit of information. This is how intentions get misinterpreted. It leads to people on both sides making assumptions about the other's motivations, and it makes for a rancorous, hostile environment, which is precisely what happened in 2010.

It was October 13, and the Obama White House, via the Offices of Public Engagement and Urban Affairs, hosted the first African American Online Summit. Organizers at the White House touted the summit as a four-hour policy briefing and discussion for leaders in the African American online media world and blogosphere. It was aimed at highlighting the accomplishments of the Obama Administration. They stressed that there was an "on-the-ground" need to let people know the importance of the midterm elections and beyond (as in the then-upcoming Presidential Elections in 2012) and to highlight the Obama Administration's initiatives on issues important to urban and Black communities, "such as jobs, the economy, health care, education, community investment, civil rights and civil liberties, and the First Lady's Let's Move initiative." Those invited included reporters from specialty media outlets both large and small, such as BET Networks, *Essence*, and prominent blogs such as *The Root, ConcreteLoop*, and others.

Many of the reporters saw this as an opportunity to get relevant policy directly from the principal—a rare occurrence in White House media relations. The inclusion of bloggers was definitely a new twist, but not surprising since this President was known for his new media tech savvy. We saw this during his campaign when his organizers effectively used the Internet and social networks to win the hearts and minds of previously ignored or uninvolved young voters. Obama made it clear that he wanted Black bloggers at the summit because he felt "The black blogosphere was a crucial medium through which the White House could convey its message and get feedback from the Black community."

What did strike some as odd, though, was that while these kinds of policy meetings with niche media do occur, they aren't common at the White House. More often than not, they are conducted surreptitiously with little information about the agenda or even the invitation list leaking to the press. Yet despite the Obama White House's usually tight rein on the press, the event was touted as the first of more to come.

The President's remarks were deftly described on October 13, 2010, in an article by *New York Times* reporter Jeremy W. Peters. His report was featured in the Media and Advertising segment of the Business Section and was titled

"White House Meeting for Black Journalists Doesn't Stay Off-the-Record for Long." Peters's article quoted Obama as saying, "Part of what's so powerful about the Web is that it's not just a one-way conversation. And what that then means is we have the capacity potentially to get information about how people are thinking, what their concerns are, what's working, what's not in the way that allows us to do our job better," and adding, "We're very excited about the possibility of our interaction." As interesting as this was, it was the response by many of those in attendance that really made cyber news that day.

It seems that not everyone was 100 percent on board with the idea of being a conduit for White House propaganda. Still others viewed the invitation with skepticism, but were loath to miss the chance for a face-to-face with senior officials or the first Black American President. As it turned out, President Obama and Senior Advisor Valerie Jarrett did happen to drop by and make a few remarks, but several of the reporters remained unmoved. According to attendee Leutisha Stills's October 13, 2010, account featured on the blog *Jack & Jill Politics*, "We essentially told the White House that we are not willing to be 'pimped.' Oh, we used better articulation, but it was direct and could not be taken out of context, misunderstood or ignored."

The reporters also had issues with the tight control of information at the summit. When the reporters were invited, they were told that there would be a policy briefing and discussion, but once at the summit, they were told that what they learned during the first part of the summit could only be featured "on background"—that is, none of the officials present could be quoted for attribution. While some bristled at this restriction, what really got many of the reporters' hackles up was that they were told that any other information communicated to them during the second part of the summit was entirely off the record. In defiance, many of them posted excerpts, impressions, and photos of the event as an attempt to send a clear message to the White House that they were not going to be left out of the loop anymore.

Years of being ignored or used by politicians have also taken their toll on specialty media, as was evident in the almost universal reaction to perceived slights. What is frustrating for specialty media is that they don't get taken seriously by everyone and thus have to fight just to get noticed. The White House Correspondents' Association continuously protests to the White House about lack of access, but not much ever changes. Despite President Obama's presence, some in the group felt that they had been invited not because they could offer valuable input at the policy table but because they could give the White House better access to Black audiences. The specter of anonymity had once again reared its ugly head, despite the event being devoted entirely to Black media.

As proof of this affront, the summit itself didn't receive any advanced coverage, and the mainstream broadcast media never noticed it because of the resulting defiance of the ban on reporting. It seems that first specialty media, and now Black online media, are to be given short shrift by everyone from the White House to the large mainstream media. Once again our voices will be silent during policy debates and discussions that directly impact our communities. It begs the question: "Did the White House even notice that although the summit was a first of its kind, other media chose not to cover it at all?" I think not. This just once again proves that stories about Blacks, Black issues, or significant historical events that involve Blacks are often not considered important or sexy enough to cover.

We only get put on the front burner if our demographic suddenly becomes politically important to the White House. That's because the Communications Office at the White House is more concerned about getting its message out to as many people as possible. And it's why the guys in the front row of the Briefing Room are so important.

Literally and figuratively, the Communications Office at the White House is the President's voice. In general, the staff of the Communications Office are the word guys. They are the people the President turns to when he needs to articulate his vision. They are also the speechwriters and staffers who develop communications or media strategies, not just at the White House, but across the administration. Coherence, consistency, "staying on message"—these are all part of the work of the Communications Office. They also perform public outreach and work with various constituencies. For example, there is a Director of Specialty Media, and this is the person the President turns to when getting out the word on initiatives and more.

If, however, he needs someone to make announcements and handle and respond to reporters' inquiries, he often will turn to the Press Secretary, which is why the never-ending pas de deux continues between reporters and the Press Secretary. As long as access to the President during Q&A is tightly controlled and primarily doled out to the biggest media, we will continue to try to curry the favor of the Press Secretary in the hope of getting even a small advantage over our competitors. We are the curse that plagues every Press Secretary and President. Our day-to-day inquiries about accountability may seem rude, intrusive, and ill-timed, but they are the price every President must pay for the privilege of governing in a democracy. For those of us in specialty media, our burden is the constant struggle to stand out from the crowd and not be left on the periphery.

On October 6, 2003, the fanfare was typical for the Official White House State Visit of Kenya's President, but the mood was off. Everyone from admin-

istration officials to the press was waiting to hear from Pre
current controversy befalling him—the Central Intelligence
investigation. Attention, even minimally, was not focused on
as they were trying to work through issues of terrorism and
peace process, among other things.

Knowing this going into the event, some White House staffers in the lower press office had devised a plan to make this event rise to the level of other state visits. The plan was executed—racial window dressing—and I was the unsuspecting operative to carry it out. At midday the historic East Room filled with reporters of all ethnicities waiting for the joint press conference between President Bush and Kenyan President Kibaki.

My caramel brown hue, a shade of beautiful Africa Black, put me center stage, not with the American Press Corps but with my fellow brother and sister reporters from Africa.

This had never happened to me before, leading me to believe that strategic placement was what they were most concerned about. Six years into the White House beat, I had dealt with issues of racial diversity from inaction to action. Nothing could top this. Race was the overriding theme of this White House, creating a dark backdrop that left black and blue bruising on my emotions. I was the only Black American to question the President that day. That is not odd as there are just a few Blacks in the White House Press Corps. But this new window-dressing issue took this race issue to another level.

The reaction from the predominately White male Press Corps fraternity to include some women was a mixed bag. Some colleagues were angry or miffed, saying it only happened because "You are Black." Others thought I got called on by the President and garnered his attention, so no harm or foul done. In a very warped sense, some thought it was a badge of honor to be displayed for the day.

But I cried foul inside as I pretended outwardly not to mind. I am five generations removed from the last known slave in my family, reflecting on an American history of hundreds of years of government-sanctioned terrorism on my ancestors. So, yes I was upset. More than upset, I was beside myself, asking confidants inside and away from the White House what should I do about the egregious wrong.

Ironically, President George W. Bush, without a seating chart before him, which is not typical, discovered the faux pas and called the world's attention to his staff's insensitivity. The chiding started at the second question of the dual press conference when President Bush addressed Kenyan President Kibaki, saying, "You're welcome to call on somebody from your Press Corps, M President."

Immediately after that sentence President Bush noticed my unusual seating and uttered, "April, you're not in his Press Corps. You're trying to play like you're in his Press Corps." There was a smattering of nervous laughter.

The White House transcript for that day was telling, except my comments were sometimes inaudible and were not attributed to me directly. My words coming from a sense of embarrassment and hurt were only seen as a questioner, with a "Q" before any explanation as to why I was there.

Q: They put me over here.

PRESIDENT BUSH: I know, but this is subversion and this isn't— (laughter.)

What the microphones failed to transmit for the transcript is my retort, "I am not trying to subvert anything; this is not political and I was assigned this seat by your staff."

"W," the man who in some ways contradicted his own philosophy of everyone being on a level playing field, spotted the problem. He thought it odd, that I, a well-recognized member of the White House Press Corps, be given the distinction of being put into the foreign press section for the State Visit of the President of Kenya. Those reporters (except for one in that section) were Black and Brown, and there were three White American White House Correspondents who sat next to me, thinking I sat there on my own. I guess the general thought was that I fit in perfectly. For the record, this had never happened to me in my years of covering the White House. Maybe it was a slip by the White House that reflected a thought, of Marcus Garvey's Back to Africa Movement. Better yet, the thought might have even been that I could feel comfortable with my own color and those sharing a similar ancestry. I was honored to be with those of my heritage as I am part of that rich history, but what was denied me was the other side, the distinction of being an American, too.

The reality told to me by press office staffers was that I was not sitting in the standard seating area for the Press Corps but for foreign press. Days later, still a bit miffed by my seating, the lower press office told me they did me "a favor so I could get called on." That discussion began from a joke I gave to those in the press office that placed me in the seat. I asked, now that Governor Arnold Schwarzenegger will be visiting the White House a bit more, "Where will you [put me, in the Europe]an section?" The persons in the lower press office took [offense at the commen]t and then began to explain that I should be grateful that [someone thought o]f me for my seating.

[My race didn']t seem to be a concern for President Bush. I got called on [often in the roo]m, the side, as well as the front. But on this occasion my

seating was of utmost concern to the lower press office. I was
window dressing at best. They did me a favor all right! I was not only called ~
but the President interrupted the press conference three times because he did
not understand why I was seated in the brotherhood and sisterhood of Kenyan
journalists. He thought I was trying to take advantage of my God-given coloring
by sitting in that section. President Bush even tried to get the Kenyan President
to call on me after he realized he was making a public show out of his staffer's
mistake.

PRESIDENT BUSH: April, are you going to try again to look like you're in the—be care-
ful. (Laughter.) Mr. President, call on who you— (laughter.)
PRESIDENT KIBAKI: Yes, yes.
PRESIDENT BUSH: I exposed you. (Laughter.)

President Kibaki did not pick my brown hand in the second row, opting for
a question from the front. What was inaudible is that I told President Bush that
he needed to call on me so I could formally ask a question at the joint press conference. There was a third presidential pronouncement of my attempts to get a
question answered while in the Kenyan press section.

PRESIDENT BUSH: April, you're really beginning to bother the President. (Laughter.)
PRESIDENT KIBAKI: No, no. (Laughter.)
PRESIDENT BUSH: Okay, I am anxious to hear what you've got to say. Go ahead. Let
her rip.
Q: Thank you so much.
PRESIDENT BUSH: Yes, April.
Q: Mr. President, on another issue, the CIA leak-gate. What is your confidence level in
the results of the DOJ investigation about any of your staffers not being found guilty or
being found guilty? And what do you say to critics of the administration who say that this
administration retaliates against naysayers?
PRESIDENT BUSH: First of all, I'm glad you brought that question up. This is a very seri-
ous matter, and our administration takes it seriously. As members of the Press Corps here
know, I have, at times, complained about leaks of security information, whether the leaks
be in the legislative branch or in the executive branch. And I take those leaks very seriously.
   And, therefore, we will cooperate fully with the Justice Department. I've got all the
confidence in the world the Justice Department will do a good, thorough job. And that's
exactly what I want them to do, is a good, thorough job. I'd like to know who leaked, and
if anybody has got any information inside our government or outside our government who
leaked, you ought to take it to the Justice Department so we can find out the leaker.

I have told my staff, I want full cooperation with the Justice Department. And when they ask for information, we expect the information to be delivered on a timely basis. I expect it to be delivered on a timely basis. I want there to be full participation, because, April, I am most interested in finding out the truth.

And, you know, there's a lot of leaking in Washington, D.C. It's a town famous for it. And if this helps stop leaks of—this investigation in finding the truth, it will not only hold someone to account who should not have leaked—and this is a serious charge, by the way. We're talking about a criminal action, but also hopefully will help set a clear signal we expect other leaks to stop, as well. And so I look forward to finding the truth.

Q: What about retaliation? People are saying that it's retaliation—

PRESIDENT BUSH: I don't know who leaked the information, for starters. So it's hard for me to answer that question until I find out the truth. You hear all kinds of rumors. And the best way to clarify the issue is for full participation with the Justice Department.

These are professionals who are professional prosecutors who are leading this investigation, and we look forward to—look, I want to know. I want to know, and the best way to do this is for there to be a good, thorough investigation, which, apparently, is going to happen soon. And all I can tell you is inside the White House, we've said, gather all the information that's requested and get it ready to be analyzed by the Justice Department.

Listen, thank you all very much. Mr. President, I'm glad you're here.

PRESIDENT KIBAKI: Very good.

PRESIDENT BUSH: Appreciate it.

PRESIDENT KIBAKI: Thank you very much.

PRESIDENT BUSH: Thank you, sir.

~~It was overtly racial on a very personal level~~. For the record, I do not consider anyone in the Bush Administration a racist. In this case, perception is not reality. I just think if you are not surrounded by or understand a culture, you will make hurtful mistakes in policy and for cameras to see, like this one. Realizing what he did that day, President Bush spoke of the incident at the opulent, formally attired Kenyan State Dinner that night. I happened to be a guest of the President with an invitation from weeks prior for the auspicious occasion. That night, while in the receiving line and with Mrs. Bush present, the President said, "I was a bit feisty there today." I said, "Yes," agreeing with his toned-down assessment. His comeback was basically that he likes me and "jokes with me like that as some others in the Press Corps could not take it."

Andy Card, the President's Chief of Staff, even commented on the several-hours-old Press Office gaff, agreeing, "It was bad!"

I moved the topic of conversation to what I thought was a more comfortable subject to take the elephant out of the room. I thanked President Bush for the invitation to the State Dinner, saying, "It means so much being five generations removed from a slave to be your guest at the White House."

He literally jumped in shock and said, "Keep your objectivity now."

My response was, "For sure."

Change in my reporting style would never happen as I continue to see discrepancies in actions at the Executive Mansion. Some reporters would even wear the President's comments from the dinner as a badge of honor. It was a double-edged sword to gain the recognition some would call Washington power, a platinum reporter status, and for others to be singled out for my race made me think back to the civil rights marches of the 1960s for equality. The majesty of the Kenyan visit was all but dismissed that day. The largeness of the Kenyan issues were diminished as this dual press conference progressively worsened. My thoughts moved back and forth between the Press Corps flight over Kenya during the 2003 presidential visit to Africa and the East Room event.

Intentional or unintentional, the President again basically bypassed Kenya. The first time was in the summer of 2003. Concerns for the President's safety during his 2003 five-nation Africa tour left us flying over the East African nation. We never touched down for a President-to-President discussion of substantive issues of antiterrorism, the Sudan peace process, other regional issues (perhaps Somalia and Congo, Burundi), as well as internal political and economic reform efforts in Kenya. HIV/AIDS in Africa could also have been a major topic of discussion at the meeting. With that knowledge, some of the continent's news headlines read: "We Have Enough Bushes in Africa," and "Bush on Safari." They basically criticized the reason for the visit and lack of substance. Kenya could have been that point as the trip was bogged down by controversy over the President's State of the Union speech and sixteen words on Iraq and "yellowcake" (a type of uranium considered a step in the development of nuclear weapons). Some White House staffers even joked that it was "the trip that wasn't."

With Kenya cut from the tour list, the presidential air convoy gave us a consolation prize by flying over the highest mountain in Africa. The plane conveniently flew over the Tanzania and Nairobi, Kenya, area, the cradle of Mt. Kilimanjaro, the highest point on the African continent. At the time, to fly by this majestic snow-capped peak, considered one of the largest in the world, was a good trade-off. But now, as Kenya was short-changed at home and on American soil, it is obvious they deserved better.

That historic Africa trip did produce a stowaway on board the press charter for that several-hour flight from South Africa to Uganda. Ironically, the unidentified man who called Soweto home took a seat in the back of the press charter, just to the left and in front of the Secret Service in the back of the plane. He was not discovered until touchdown in Uganda. He was treated like a hard-pass-carrying member of the Press Corps. He was even served a spinach frittata for breakfast. After apprehending this fellow outside of the presidential event at a resort on Lake Victoria, the Secret Service said the President was never in any danger. I'm not so sure about that. The man was about one hundred yards from where the President was speaking. Thank God nothing happened!

Minority groups by race, gender, and sexual orientation have demonstrated, even more so lately, that they are a large voting block that cannot be denied. During the 2012 presidential election process, President Obama pointed out that specialty media would have worked to Mitt Romney's advantage, as Obama said in an off-the-record discussion with reporters that he would win the presidential election again because Mitt Romney has alienated Hispanics. Pew Research showed that President Obama was right. Latinos voted for President Obama over Mitt Romney by 71 percent to 27 percent. Romney also alienated the Black community, and there his numbers were much worse. President Obama received a lower percentage of the White vote and still won the election. According to the *Washington Post* article "Mitt Romney's Neglect of Black Americans Failed Him at the Polls" by Crystal Wright on November 7, 2012, President Obama only received 38 percent of the White vote, down five points from 2008.

NBC News Decision 2012 Presidential Election Results on race shows:

	Obama	Romney	% Total
White	39	59	72
Black	93	6	13
Hispanic/Latino	71	27	10
Asian	73	26	3
Other	58	38	2

There will always be varying reasons as to why someone casts a ballot for a candidate. But the equation when votes are cast generally adds up to voting for the person who best represents your ideas or whom you think can move this country forward with you in mind. There will always be a contrasting of some sort, but with this President the differences of political ideology are in stark contrast to the McCain/Palin ticket and even the Romney/Ryan ticket. The example is in a June 2012 Presidential Campaign bus tour ride with Governor Mitt Romney in Frankenmuth, Michigan. He held a twenty-minute meeting with three Black reporters and a producer for an off-the-record (OTR) discussion on issues pertaining to the Black community. Those joining the Romney 2012 Presidential Campaign bus tour in Frankenmuth, Michigan, were T. J. Holmes, James Blue, Perry Bacon, and yours truly, April Ryan. Unfortunately, the conversation could not be reported since it was identified as OTR.

In fact, Governor Mitt Romney in 2012 gave only two on-the-record interviews to African Americans in the media, and one was Oprah Winfrey. But his one and only interview with the Black press was to Derek Dingle of *Black Enterprise* magazine. Dingle conducted the interview at the NAACP Convention where Romney addressed the crowd. At that same convention, Romney's speech drew loud boos and hisses when he said he would repeal Obamacare. After the speech he met with Dingle. Romney was asked, "How would your presidential cabinet look?" Romney said, "I would love to have a cabinet that reflected the fabric of America."

But now that the event is over and the OTR has expired, I can tell you what happened. I asked Romney what he thought he could do to lower the Black unemployment rate. This very accomplished businessman replied back, "I don't understand."

But, *Black Enterprise* got the question on the record. "If you're elected, where do you expect to see the unemployment rate?" His answer, "I see it being 6% or less by the end of my [first] term." Some in the Black media who have complained about Romney's lack of on-the-record access say this is consistent with his infamous "47 percent and gifts" comment. In contrast, according to Dr. Kumar, President Obama had given an interview to Oprah Winfrey and he had also participated in over thirty-five interviews with Black media since his official early April reelection bid. During a campaign interview with *The Tom Joyner Morning Show*, the President conveyed confidence in an election win, saying, "After the election I will have won my last race."

So even as specialty media is needed and yet relegated to a hurry-up-and-wait status until an administration thinks it is time to dust us off the shelf, it is hard for many of us to be patient. We have a job to do. There is a reason so few of the minority media outlets cover the White House daily. For over forty years American Urban Radio has been the only news outlet with a booth and a seat in the White House Briefing Room. That room is not forgiving to those who are not there all day, every day, coveting that highly regarded golden space.

There are often public displays of members of Black media coming to the White House from time to time through the years, but they are not there every day. I wish that dynamic would change. It did for about a year when Barack Obama became President. There was a picture taken for *Ebony* magazine at the beginning of the Obama Administration. There were folks there I had never seen before, and some of us jokingly said, "I wonder who will be standing at the end of the four years?" Unfortunately, those numbers quickly dwindled back to just one. It is sad to say that it is primarily me day in and day out in that room representing all of Black media.

That's why I take my job so seriously.

4

PRESIDENTS AND RACE

Throughout history, politicians have dodged the issue of race with the skill and finesse of a trained boxer. Instead of facing the topic head on, they have become increasingly adept at bobbing and weaving their way around the issue. Those who run for President are the heavyweight champs when it comes to the skill of racial avoidance. It's unfortunate that in our society, and especially in the world of politics, we have accepted the fact that politicians will most likely dance around an issue, especially a difficult one, instead of providing a solid, actionable plan.

Out of all American Presidents, only a select few have made even an attempt to broach the subject of racial inequality in this country. What they don't realize is that the American public would much rather know where Presidents stand on an issue than feel as if they are afraid to commit to something so important. At least then people would be aware of what the politician believes instead of having to read between the lines of a carefully worded speech and heavily edited public comments. According to Dr. Kumar, "The presidency has been a crucial institution on issues of race because it is through presidential action that many things have come about."

The few times that executive power has been used to address race it has created a noticeable shift in the racial dynamics in this country. A perfect example is when President Eisenhower enforced the Supreme Court decision to desegregate Central High School in Little Rock. Dr. Kumar said, "He [Eisenhower] federalized the [National] Guard in Arkansas and they became federal troops to help make certain that those schools, that the courts had ordered in *Cooper vs. Aaron*, that those schools be desegregated. And it took presidential action;

Congress wasn't the one acting. The courts did what they could, but it took presidential enforcement and that has often been the case, so the presidency is seen as a place where actions happen on race. For example, it was Truman who desegregated the armed forces; Wilson called for an Equal Opportunity Commission. It was President Kennedy who got involved in issues of education and race, and also voting."

Of course, the current public attitude and cultural climate also dictates the time when a potentially divisive policy will have a chance of being accepted. According to Dr. Jeff Gardere, Assistant Professor, Behavioral Medicine at Touro College of Osteopathic Medicine in New York City, "Discussing race and politics could work against us, especially if we're trying to point out to people what may be going on as far as either conscious or unconscious racism or even institutional racism. People are very uncomfortable with that and I think when you bring that up, the fear is that you might be labeled as an agitator or troublemaker or someone who might be dangerous with regard to being perhaps litigious or gumming up the works, if you will."

That agitation has always been a catalyst for change in the movement. The push for parity, particularly in the South, began to take shape allowing for Black flight into higher socioeconomic classes and a better way of life than what had become the status quo. The fight was for basic equality in accommodations, voting rights, pay, education, transportation, and other areas with disparities. When asked if a modern-era White House needs to take the civil rights movement's historical impact into account, President Jimmy Carter's UN ambassador Andrew Young said, "They should take it. Any White House has to take it into account."

Reverend Jesse Jackson Sr. was also one of those making a deliberate choice to push the envelope on changing the racist laws in this country. "Well, many of them [Presidents] embraced Dr. King as a martyr, but not as a marcher. As a marcher he said his job was to make the comforted disturbed, and disturb the comfortable. He shook things up. He kept mass action, applying pressure. We got public accommodations because we all applied pressure to Democratic administrations—the right to vote, the EEOC, contract compliance, Vietnam— because he [Dr. King] felt it was his job to be at once personable with them, but not so close as to forsake his first responsibility to get the leadership to change the course of the government."

The way Reverend Jackson views it, "Dr. King has been the most pivotal force in American history." Jackson says life in America is often divided based on historical occurrences, such as the years before Dr. King and after King's murder in Memphis on April 4, 1968. He contends, "You've got life in America almost before and after Dr. King. You've got before and after Abe Lincoln. Before Civil War, after Civil War. The slavery question and the Union."

During his time as President, Abraham Lincoln had on occasion met with abolitionist Frederick Douglass on the relationship of emancipation, Black soldiers, and the Union victory surrounding the Civil War. Douglass found Lincoln receptive, as he noted that he was not "vain of pomp and ceremony."

Reverend Jackson also says, "King—you had before and after King on the issue of legal Jim Crow. They are the transformative forces. You probably got three tall trees: Lincoln, Johnson, and Dr. King. No President used his authority with more power of change than Lyndon Johnson. Lincoln, because of Civil War, yes, but . . . Johnson as President. [Johnson's] 1964 Civil Rights Act, 1965 Voting Rights Act, speech at Howard University, he was a transformative figure. And Democrats ran kind of shy of Johnson. All the rights we now enjoy came under Johnson, and he laid the groundwork for the Great Society, War on Poverty, that's Lyndon Johnson."

Former head of the U.S. Commission on Civil Rights, Mary Frances Berry, also identified the same three, saying, "Well, if you're talking about Presidents, obviously, Lincoln and LBJ would be pillars because there's nobody that's been as strong on civil rights since reconstruction, as LBJ was, and I don't know, it's just that Black people don't appreciate that." So while Johnson was able to use his power to implement real change in our racial landscape, he may not always get as much recognition because most people felt it was long overdue. Regardless of that fact, he was the one President unafraid of committing to the issue of inequality in the United States.

Andrew Young remembered attending a meeting with President Johnson and Dr. King on the issue of voting rights, and the President gave meeting participants little to expect in regard to its passage. The meeting occurred several months after the passage of the Civil Rights Act. Racial tension was at an all-time high as the bodies of three men (two White and one Black), who had been attempting to register African Americans to vote, were found in Mississippi. "I was in the meeting with Lyndon Johnson and MLK in December of 1964 and it was about the 15th of December, and he spent about an hour and half explaining why he could not introduce the Voting Rights Act. He just didn't have the power. He just didn't have the votes, the influence, and we walked out of the meeting, and Martin said, 'I guess we have to find a way to give the President some power.' I mean, just let it drop like that . . . and the next week, Amelia Boynton came to visit us from Selma and told us what they were going through in terms of denial of their voting rights."

According to Young, the plotting began to encourage the President to change his mind on the important issue of voting rights. So while Johnson did play a key role in implementing real change, it wasn't always part of his agenda. At the Civil Rights Summit on April 10, 2014, in honor of Lyndon Baines Johnson and the fiftieth anniversary of the Civil Rights Act, President Barack Obama said of Johnson, "During his first twenty years in Congress, he opposed every Civil Rights Bill that came up for a vote, once calling the push for federal legislation a farce and a sham." President Obama said President Johnson was picked as a vice-presidential running mate because he could deliver the White, southern vote. Obama said that at the beginning of the Kennedy Administration, Johnson "cautioned" Kennedy about "racial controversy."

African American Democratic South Carolina Congressman James Clyburn describes the complicated recipe for success on Capitol Hill. "I think that's the way you do things in Washington. You have to decide what it is you don't mind giving up to get whatever it is you want to get. I think that people make the mistake. I try to advise people all the time—you got to really make people want to vote for you, people want to support you. You just can't go out and make people just do things. I see people all the time just go out and coerce. It doesn't work well. . . . especially when you're in an organized caucus because people's feelings very easily get hurt. You have to be very careful."

So after implementation of the Civil Rights Act, activists felt the time was right to push for voting rights, but once again, racial climate and attitudes played a key role. This time it was a matter of pure logistics. They had difficulty establishing a place to have a meeting in the state of Alabama on how to make change happen. Young said Blacks "could not walk down the street to have an NAACP meeting in a church. It was illegal. There was a local Alabama injunction against more than three people walking down the street [together]."

However, with enough momentum and enough support, almost anything can happen, and ultimately an NAACP meeting was held in early January. Young was there. "We knew we were breaking those injunctions. And we knew we were challenging the whole system of Alabama, and saw this as a path to giving the President the power to do something we felt he wanted to do. It took five or six deaths and six months of nonviolent demonstrations, but that's a small price to pay for the Voting Rights Act and the changes that came." Although the violence-free movement was making history and picking up momentum, it suffered a catastrophic, almost crippling loss. As Young recalled, "We were well on the way, but the assassination of MLK and Robert Kennedy six weeks apart shook up the movement. So we've never really quite recovered from that."

The assassinations of Dr. King and Robert Kennedy were a real blow to the progress being made because these two powerful men had given people, especially Black folks, something they weren't used to. Hope. But when Dr. King was murdered at the Lorraine Motel in Memphis, Tennessee, on April 4, 1968, and Bobby Kennedy was killed on June 6 in the kitchen of the Ambassador Hotel on a campaign stop in Los Angeles, California, that brief ray of hope was quickly stolen away. The movement was back to square one, and there was only one man who could possibly help pull that nation out of its slump and back on track. That was the President of the United States. Regardless of the fact that Johnson had to be persuaded on voting rights, he eventually picked up President Kennedy's equality baton and carried it farther than Kennedy had probably even initially planned.

Dr. Martha Joynt Kumar proudly and enthusiastically marched with Dr. King and many others during the civil rights movement, showing that there were plenty of Whites who also thought equality was an important issue. "After Kennedy's death and Lyndon Johnson decided to make the Civil Rights Act of 1964 be a monument to President Kennedy, and he took a very stern view of what needed to be done . . . It wasn't just that you should reward schools that desegregate, instead what you would do is go after and punish those districts that did not *desegregate*. And in addition to that, public accommodations, all public accommodations, that are involved in any way, in interstate commerce, like being near a federal highway, that they were going to be covered, and that you couldn't discriminate on the basis of race. When it came to voting rights, Eisenhower was involved, but ultimately Lyndon Johnson signed the 1965 Voting Rights Act, which is really one of the most important and successful pieces of legislation in the twentieth century," she said. "It really brought about equality of voting in the South, and of course presidential action also was involved in making certain that everyone could vote, in terms of no literacy test and that sort of thing. So we are used to Presidents being at the vanguard because sometimes it's just a matter of taking a particular action. So we look to Presidents for issues of leadership on issues of race. I think that's a natural thing. But the issues of race today are much more difficult to get at. For example, the disparity in unemployment figures."

Sometimes, it's easy to forget that during this turbulent time, activists and civil rights supporters were constantly under the threat of possible harm. As demonstrated by the horrific deaths of the three men in Mississippi, politicians and high-profile leaders weren't the only ones in danger. It's an amazing test of their dedication and focus that enlightened Blacks and Whites continued to push for change. After the horrific and violent deaths of King and Kennedy, the movement was at a pivotal juncture. It was becoming increasingly difficult to maintain morale and hope. However, Ambassador Young says that if the pair had not died so soon, everyone would have benefitted by their policies. According to Young, King and Bobby Kennedy came to an understanding about the realities of America in the 1960s. "Bobby Kennedy and Martin Luther King had come to a consensus almost on poverty, and it wasn't Black poverty. I mean it was poverty. It was Indian poverty. It was White-Appalachian poverty. It was poverty of the central cities, and the welfare state. Both of them [Kennedy and King] had a sense of conscious about America, and they were both totally unselfish."

A major reason why Blacks as a group have not been able to climb the next rung up the middle-class ladder and beyond is because economically the weight of the Black community is not collective in pushing a movement or policy on their behalf. Also, Blacks as a whole do not have the financial status of other groups, and in American politics money always commands the attention of lawmakers. Black former Virginia Governor Doug Wilder contends, "There is a one-word definition for politics and that is money."

When you look at the economic empowerment of Blacks in general, there has never been parity. The inequality began with slavery, and today the effects of that policy over two hundred years ago manifests itself in the jobless numbers in which Blacks are almost twice as likely not to have a job as the majority of this country. According to Young, "Dr. King said, in part of the March on Washington speech—that nobody quotes—that 'American Negroes were presented with a promissory note' and when [they] presented it at the bank of justice of freedom and opportunity, the promissory note came back marked insufficient funds. He went on to say, 'I refuse to believe that the bank of justice is bankrupt. I still have a dream.' So *the dream* is what everyone has latched on to, but the dream was about social-economic equality."

Today, a high concentration of African Americans live in urban, densely populated communities that are not considered "wealth areas." In 2014, a report by Stephen Ohlemacher of the Associated Press shows that the richest population in America is the 12th Congressional District in New York City. The average income for those residents was over $75,000 a year, per person. The U.S. Census Bureau reported in 2009 the average overall household income for all Americans, regardless of race, was $49,777. The average household income for Asian and Pacific Islanders was $65,469. The household income for Whites that year, $51,861. The household income for Hispanics that year was $38,039. And finally, the household income for Blacks was $32,584.

Blacks, documented as the poorest economic group in the nation, have been once again relegated to "the back of the bus" because of the lack of access to political capital, money, and subsequently power. The 1970s were relatively quiet on race compared to the two preceding decades. In fact, it was so uneventful that when then-President Gerald Ford delivered his State of the Union speech, he did not give mention to Black America, or even urban America for that matter. Then–National Urban League President Vernon Jordan took action and started the organization's own annual report, the "State of Black America."

After President Ford left office, a southern President was ushered into the White House, and he knew from personal experience how racial problems were affecting our country. President Jimmy Carter publicly stepped into the debate by addressing the failed policies of integration. Carter did not think Blacks should lose their ethnic identity, saying, "I don't think government ought to deliberately try to break down an ethnically oriented neighborhood by artificially injecting into it someone from another ethnic group just to create some form of integration."

Today, integration and gentrification are occurring, and it's spurred by sheer economics. Whites are moving into traditionally Black, urban areas such as Harlem, New York; Washington, D.C.; and Baltimore, Maryland, after the Great Recession totally changed the real estate landscape. There are many economic benefits to locating and improving homes in neighborhoods in need of upgrades. It's something Carter was encouraging during his tenure.

While the nation's seventh President, Andrew Jackson, was the first to open up the White House to the general public, Carter took it further by inviting Blacks to a place they had previously never considered accessible. Ernie Green, one of the Little Rock Nine who integrated Central High School in Arkansas in the 1960s, was also the Assistant Secretary of Labor in the Carter Administration. He said, "For African Americans, the White House is a mystery . . . I think [President] Carter was really just the beginning for African Americans paying interest to the inner workings of the White House. The Carter Administration had some of the first numbers, at the time they were small, African Americans having staff jobs of any significance." Unfortunately that inclusion momentum was short-lived.

Ronald Reagan did not endear himself to Black lawmakers during his eight years at the helm. Former New York 11th District Congressman Ed Towns served three decades in Congress. He was the first Black to serve as head of the Oversight and Government Reform Committee, and he worked with five Presidents after becoming a congressman during the Reagan Administration. Towns recalled that members of the Congressional Black Caucus (CBC) had few meetings with President Reagan. When those meetings did occur, CBC members and White House staffers would often ultimately take over the sessions because

President Reagan would fall asleep. "If you are not interested, it is hard to stay awake," Towns said. He remembers there were staffers in the meeting who would lead the meetings as Reagan slept. "He would slap himself on the face to wake himself up, reminding himself to wake up or saying to himself, 'What are you doing?'" With a smile in his voice, Towns says the "job of the President is a taxing position. One way to look at it."

Bishop T. D. Jakes, CEO and Senior Pastor of Potter's House and TDJ Enterprises, reflected on the lack of some past presidential connections with the Black community. "Any time people feel hopeless and helpless and segregated from the decision makers, I think an aloofness has developed, where the political moves are not about you." Jakes believes decades later that has changed to an extent. "I do think the Obama Administration marked a very significant difference, and African Americans watched far more intently."

But Bishop Jakes makes clear that the issue does not just lie with those in power. The Black community must also take responsibility. He says, "We are absolutely part of the problem. Any time we get people elected, and then we don't hold them accountable and we sit back and watch what's happening in the country then we're a part of the problem, and not the solution. I think we should hold all elected officials accountable. This notion that African Americans should hold the Congressional Black Caucus accountable is a limited notion. It's not just Black officials. We should hold all officials accountable."

Eight years of President Reagan and then another four with President George Herbert Walker Bush left minorities with images of folks like Reverend Jesse Jackson demonstrating outside of the White House, demanding to be let inside for a seat at the table. It was a time when President Reagan vetoed a bill calling for sanctions in South Africa. President Reagan was joined by British Prime Minister Margaret Thatcher, who also did not support sanctions. The African National Congress, better known as the ANC, was placed on the State Department's terrorist list. With a nation full of Black Americans watching, it was apparent that other countries were trying to work through their own racial issues. South Africa was one of the richest nations in the world. Much of the wealth came from the labor force that was relegated to pennies for pay. As Governor Wilder stated, politics and money are linked for better or worse. "There are those who support the 1964 Public Accommodations Bill reluctantly, but still they were supporting South African apartheid which is nothing but American apartheid transferred to South Africa."

Ultimately, the Black electorate is a savvy voting bloc, understanding that no one will be that savior for one race. Instead, you must vote for the person you believe will address at least some of the needs of the community as a whole. The percentage of Blacks voting for a Republican candidate has dropped dramatically since the 1956 Eisenhower/Nixon ticket received 39 percent of the Black vote according to the 2008 Democratic Convention Guide. As an about-face, the Black vote began to move in unison in 1964 with 94 percent of the vote for LBJ. A whopping 85 percent of the Black vote helped to put Jimmy Carter in the White House. Fast forward to George W. Bush and his first run for the office in 2000. He received 8 percent of the Black vote, and in 2004 it was up to 11 percent. The numbers have become anemic, and at a blistering pace. In 2008, John McCain only received about 3 percent of the vote against Barack Obama. The numbers did climb a bit to 6 percent for Mitt Romney.

Black former Republican Party Chair Michael Steele believes, "Unless people are medically color-blind, people will always notice race. Black politicians certainly do rise to national heights, but how the race is viewed, and for that matter, used for or against them depends on which side of the aisle they're on. The reality is that Black conservatives are still treated as political anomaly at best, and traitors to their community at worst. This makes things difficult sometimes, but the greatness of our country and our political system is that nothing is impossible."

Each decade has brought pivotal change to the push toward equity, but where is the focus now? "Economic disparities for low-income, minority children is the civil rights issue of the twenty-first century," Steele said. "As long as we trap our children in failing government schools, they will never have an equal shot in life. The other problems flow from that as well—dropouts and subsequent incarceration or teen pregnancy, HIV/AIDS and drug use, unemployment. Now, that's not to say that deep cultural issues relating to family breakdown aren't equally important here, because schools can only do so much if a family environment is working against a child. But the government doesn't run families, so we can't do quite as much there the way we can with schools. Let's start with that lower-hanging fruit and see if we can make inroads. We need to empower the parents who are motivated and want to rescue their kids from failing schools with the choices available to other Americans. Dollars should follow the child," Steele says.

History proves that change is possible and that politicians can be important allies to the Black community, but diligence and persistence are crucial. If the activists of the 1960s showed us anything, it's that we can't wait around for change to happen. We can't assume that others will take the lead or that just because we cast a vote we've done our part. Politicians answer to their constituents, and as part of that community, Blacks and all minorities need to voice their concerns.

As we all know, the buck stops with the President of the United States. Next, I'll share my interviews with key members of the Oval Office, including two Presidents, in an effort to shed light on their views on race relations in America and how it should be addressed. Once we understand where they are coming from and what they are thinking, it may be useful information going forward. Hopefully these insights will help provide some perspective and will show that things can be different and maybe even one day be equal.

While some of the challenges of our community may seem overwhelming, many of the leaders that I talked to mentioned time and again that African Americans need to take responsibility and demonstrate that, regardless of the past. We not only owe it to our enslaved ancestors and to those brave civil rights activists, we owe it to ourselves.

January 21, 2014, in the Harlem Office of William Jefferson Clinton's post interview for the book The Presidency in Black and White *(photo credit to Diane Nine).*

April Ryan greets South African President Nelson Mandela following a White House East Room event September 22, 1998, during his second state visit to the White House.

Reporting inside of the Door of No Return at Masion Des Esclaves (translated as the House of Slaves) on Goree Island, Senegal, during President Obama's June 2013 visit to Africa. This was my third time inside the Door (first with President Clinton, second with President Bush, and third with President Obama). (April Ryan private collection.)

Interview with President Barack Obama aboard Air Force One as we were flying from Senegal to South Africa June 2013. Topic of the interview was about his historic trip.

The Historic Soul Food Dinner with President Clinton and participants, July 22, 1999.

Before an Oval Office interview on Africa, we left the motorcade and President Bush suggested we wave to my fellow press colleagues, February 26, 2008.

President Clinton ended his exit interview by turning the tables and acting as if he were interviewing me in the Oval Office as I was in his chair at the Resolute Desk. November 1, 2000.

President Clinton traveled about 14 miles from my mother's family's hometown of Whiteville, North Carolina, to bridge the gap in the digital divide. The old, unused train station was his backdrop. April 26, 2000.

Interview of President George W. Bush and First Lady Laura Bush in the flying Oval Office aboard Air Force One on our way to New Orleans to view what has been done to fix the areas impacted by Katrina on the one-year anniversary of that hurricane, August 28, 2006.

President Bush and April Ryan in the Oval Office for a goodbye when Press Secretary Ari Fleischer learned it was my last day before maternity leave, May 9, 2002.

Vice President Al Gore learns a new dance besides the Macarena on board Air Force Two on the way home from the Gore Mbeki Summit in South Africa, February 19, 1999.

President Clinton walking the halls near the White House Lower Press Office eating a soft sourdough pretzel. It was the first time I ran into him in the White House and that is when I asked him to call me by my name, March 7, 1997.

The Clintons hosted a gospel concert in a tent on the South Lawn. My college choir, the Morgan State University Choir, performed. My mother and I were in attendance. After the concert, my mother wanted to meet then-First Lady Hillary Clinton, so I did what a good daughter does and made the introductions, June 3, 1998.

Each of my daughters born during the Bush Administration had their own moment with the President in the Oval Office. Here are my daughters and my dad with President Bush, July 16, 2008.

5

PRESIDENT CLINTON

January 21 was the day of one of the worst snowfalls on the East Coast in 2014. New York City was hit hard. But still my mission was to meet with former President Bill Clinton in his office in Harlem. Undeterred by the swirling blizzard, cars and people hurried by like the sky was clear. I followed suit. With snow mercilessly pounding Gotham, my agent and I hailed a cab and practically slid all the way from the Times Square area to one of the main streets of Harlem. When we were in the cab and the driver turned around, I said with excitement, "Harlem!" To my surprise the driver did not seem to share my enthusiasm. He actually did not respond at all. Wondering if he heard me, I leaned in closer to the thick plastic bulletproof divider, this time speaking much louder and forcefully. "Harlem!"

The driver, with a heavy foreign accent, said, "There is no more Harlem." With a quick retort I said, "What?" He said it is now called "Uptown!" Again I responded with, "What?" The driver said with a smile in his voice, "Yes! Harlem was bad. Blacks were killing each other. It is now called 'Uptown.'" I was not happy at all; I was actually very upset, and without thinking I leaned even closer to the divider and said, "Do you know I am Black?" Laughingly, he replied, "Yes!" Then he asked where we were from and my agent said, "Washington." I angrily said loudly and even closer to the divider that I was from "Harlem!" I asked, "Why did they change the name?" He responded, "Because of Bill Clinton."

I had seen this before, "outsiders" changing the standards in the Black community to make things more palatable or acceptable for others. Now the changes have come to Harlem. Merely because of Clinton's presence in the neighborhood, some in White America are wasting no time moving into the chocolate community with new money and big ideas. While that gentrification can be a blessing, it can also be a curse. Hard-working Black folks often find that once these areas are renovated, rents and real estate prices shoot up. Suddenly, people who grew up and raised families there are forced to move out. Another example of wealth inequality rearing its ugly head. Ironically, the history, character, and flavor of Harlem that convinced Clinton to choose that location may be in jeopardy.

Undeterred, our cab made it along icy, snow-covered 125th Street and up to the beautiful offices of the former President. After we walked inside, I stood for a moment and soaked in the spacious window that overlooked Harlem. I was still thinking about what the cabbie had said and decided to see how Mr. Clinton felt about the topic. It would also be a good icebreaker for our interview. Once seated, I asked the former President what he called the area, "Uptown or Harlem?" Clinton strategically paused as if I were asking him a trick question. But to my delight he said, "Harlem." With a sigh of relief, we were both ready for the interview.

My first glimpse inside the White House had started during the administration of William Jefferson Clinton, the forty-second President of the United States of America. The time was fraught with ambitious efforts such as health care reform, the restriction on the sale of handguns, promoting a framework for peace aimed at ending the strife in Northern Ireland, and strengthened environmental regulations. During this time the President also had to deal with the Ken Starr investigations, the Monica Lewinsky scandal, and ultimately surviving subsequent impeachment. Clinton also dispatched peacekeeping forces to war-torn Bosnia and bombed Iraq when Saddam Hussein stopped UN inspections for investigating any evidence of nuclear, chemical, and biological weapons.

Honestly, I believe before social media and the twenty-four-hour news cycle as we know it, Clinton was the original "rock star." He was something of a "bad boy," and this rock star status was perfect for the increasingly online world as the Internet began to become more of a necessity than a luxury. His personal and professional choices were ideal fodder for blogs and news websites, and those stories kept him in the public eye, for better or worse. As I covered this President, I saw in Bill Clinton a man who could walk with kings, queens, and the wealthiest in this country and beyond. Yet he was still able to connect to his core, his humble beginnings. He is the poster child for a potential men's anthem of "I'm Every Man." His journey to the highest political office is a perfect example of the American dream, growing up in the South, of modest means, in a single-parent household until his mother remarried. As is his gift now, his quick mind and easy charisma were his salvation and helped propel him to unbelievable heights, since politics relies heavily on likeability and public image.

Clinton, a centrist Democrat, was faced with many challenges, including racial issues, which dominated his White House landscape. While he was always comfortable with the topic of race (unlike many other politicians), he acknowledged that a lot of his policy and conversations on race in his second term were prodded by a Black female radio reporter. As you may have surmised, there was only one person he could be referring to—me. Clinton made that statement and more at a National Association of Black Journalists (NABJ) convention. Former Clinton Press Secretary Mike McCurry referred to my effect on the President when he said, "Power is the ability to shape and influence events, to bend history in one direction or another. Some actors have greater 'power' than others, but anyone who can bend that arc of history has the most important thing in Washington—currency and relevancy. There is no question to me that your reporting demonstrated that kind of power."

McCurry also explained that everyone in that White House had a role to play, including the press. "It helps for the rest of the White House to hear the skepticism of the press. If they aren't buying the party line, it is not likely anyone else will either. I also think good, tough questions can help expose some of the flaws in the policy. If policy is not sharp and clear, the questions in the briefing room make that abundantly clear very quickly." McCurry is the man credited with opening up the White House Briefings daily. He has since regretted his decision due to "too much posturing for the cameras on both sides. The briefing is supposed to be raw ingredients for news reporting, not news itself. The idea is that journalists take the info and check with other sources and reporting before presenting a story to the audience. Now it is an 'event' with too much attitude."

But race always played a part in the Clinton Administration in both good and bad times. President Clinton, in an exclusive interview for this book on January 21, 2014, said, "First of all, I think race still plays a part in politics. There's no question that the dominance of the very conservative Republicans in the South started as a reaction to the support of the Democrats for all of the civil rights legislation and you know, anybody who doubts that, just hadn't been paying attention."

The former President believes the only way for African Americans to obtain parity on issues in areas including jobs, housing, education, and health is to elevate the issues beyond the parties to a level where each side can come together for the common good. According to Clinton, "Lyndon Johnson said when he signed the Voting Rights Act that he was going to make the Democrats the minority party in the South for a generation . . . but it was the right thing to do and had to be done. I was very encouraged that we might begin to reverse that policy, not just for the Democratic Party, but for having a more inclusive politics. Go to the presidential election where there was Florida, for example, making a real effort to make it harder for minorities to vote . . . and . . .

April Ryan: "Al Gore?"

Bill Clinton: "Yeah, but also 2012. African Americans and Hispanics and elderly people were burden by these new rules. They just stood in line longer and waited to vote. And then this year in Virginia, the reason Terry McAuliffe won was in spite of the huge negative reaction against the health care rollout for the last ten days, they nearly beat him. The reason he won is it was the first Virginia governor's race anybody could remember where the ratio of African Americans to White voters in the governor race was exactly what it was when President Obama won a year earlier. That is, minorities started showing up at midterm as well as for the President and if that happens throughout the South. . . . For example, in Texas, if Hispanic voters voted in the same percentage as they vote in California, their turnout would increase 25 percent. So if we are equally participating in our democracy, there will be more creative cooperation between the parties and genuine outreach to all groups."

"I'll give you an example. I think the Democrats made a bad mistake by writing off low-income, small-town, and rural White voters. They used to vote for us. Now they can pass a lie detector test, if they're not racist, even those are the places that President Obama does the worse in. So I've been poking around, and I said look, it's not racist. It's culture. 'The Democrats won't do anything for us, and we don't think the Republicans will do either, but at least they're not doing anything *to* us. You want to come get our guns, and you're for gay marriage and we're not. If nobody is going to do anything for us, then we'll just vote for the people who won't do anything to us.' I think Jesse Jackson—whatever anybody wants to say about him—was the one African American leader that never, not a day in his life, would give up on poor White people. He went to Appalachia with me, remember. That night, when we had that New Markets tour, he always thought Americans who are relatively dispossessed and working as hard as they can should and could make common cost. I remember when he ran for President, in one of those races, he won South Carolina, and got 59 percent of the vote. It was an amazing coalition between African American voters and low-income White voters. He grew up there—South Carolina—and they actually believed him when he tried to get them a better deal."

"That's what America needs today. We need people talking to each other across these lines, and we need to do it whether we get votes or not. I remember when the pope made his last trip to America when I was President. He came to St. Louis. The priest in Arkansas, in Little Rock, who had been the principal of a Catholic High School for Boys, was dying of cancer. I called him, and I told him, 'I'm going to see the pope. You want to go?' I wanted him to see the pope before he died. We were really good friends, and I put quite a wager on it for the fact that he never voted for me for President because he was very much pro-life and I wasn't."

"The point is we had a real friendship. We could talk about things. We could deal with our differences. I don't want to get rid of all these differences. I just want to, you know, be able to sit down and talk to each other and get this show on the road. I think one of the things that is hurting all disposed people is that. I mean, unemployed people, low-income people, single mothers killing themselves trying to do right by their kids to get them a decent education, feed them right, not get them into this obesity epidemic and everything. It's this paralysis where everybody just goes off and gets in their bunker."

"One of the things I liked about Bush is that he'd talk to anybody. I remember when Henry Hyde tried to run me out of town—to the shock of my young White House aides—he called and asked for a meeting with himself and three or four other people to discuss an issue that was really important in his state. I gave him an appointment and nobody could believe I did it. I said, 'You don't understand. We won here. He's a member of Congress, and I want everyone to be nice to him. And when he leaves here, I want him to think we've forgotten everything he did because we gotta keep going.' We gotta keep the show on the road. . . . and I think that's what Americans need."

"I think African Americans cannot close these remaining gaps until we have a better overall economic policy, but I also think and hope that we will see a lot of attention devoted to things that will really help people succeed at home and at work. I spent a lot of time with helping people succeed at home and at work with the Family Leave Law. Welfare reform had a lot more money for childcare and for transportation and other things. We need to go back to that. We can't have people making policy just on who's voting for them. I've tried to help rural America. In rural farming states that were overwhelming Republican, I did real well when I was President. Partly, because I knew something about agriculture and I did it, and I knew they wouldn't vote for me. That wasn't what it was about. That's what we've got to get again. Once people get these jobs, we've got to try to represent everybody."

One of those analyzing the effects of race on politics is another history maker himself, former Virginia Governor Doug Wilder. Virginia's first Black governor said, "Race will always be a factor as long as people look like we look. That is not going to go away. What degree of factoring, how it surfaces or resurfaces is unimportant. When things are going well, people are not upset. The economy's good and jobs are plentiful. When we are at peace, nobody's upset with too many things. And consequently, those issues don't come to the floor. However, when you find things like what's happening in Iraq and Afghanistan, when you find the economy going south and us spending and spending and people do not have jobs . . ." That is when he believes race becomes a factor.

Clinton saw the writing on the wall and acknowledged a shift in the racial makeup in this country. The Clinton White House wanted to address the changing dynamics of a population that would begin to see a larger minority demographic. A demographic at the bottom rung of the economic pyramid was moving up the socioeconomic ladder, and it was time to prepare the nation. In February 1997 President Bill Clinton said, "Building One America is our most important mission." Simply put, it was a "heart issue" according to the President. "Money cannot buy it. Power cannot compel it. Technology cannot create it. It can only come from the human spirit."

Former Obama Administration Ambassador for Religious Freedom, Suzan Johnson Cook, served on the President's One America Race Commission as a faith advisor, remembering, "The President had seen that America was not going to be the same America, and was not the same America. So the question that we really worked around is that—Can there really be One America in the twenty-first century? And he saw that the numbers, demographically, were increasingly brown people, Latinos, and then African Americans. The power was still in White male hands for the most part. The paradigm would have to shift to deal with a shift in America, and so we didn't know what the outcome was going to be, but we were really the ones to stir the pot, got conversations going. Visited places that were having difficulties with race."

The initiative lead by the late Dr. John Hope Franklin, an African American history scholar and the author of *From Slavery to Freedom*, kept the group focused on the President's five main goals:

1. To articulate the President's vision of racial reconciliation and a just, unified America.
2. To help educate the nation about the facts surrounding the issue of race.
3. To promote a constructive dialogue, to confront and work through the difficult and controversial issues surrounding race.
4. To recruit and encourage leadership at all levels to help bridge racial divides.
5. To find, develop, and implement solutions in critical areas such as education, economic opportunity, housing, health care, crime and the administration of justice for individuals, communities, corporations, and government at all levels.

Just the idea of national White House–sponsored conversations on race left people rubbing old wounds from issues (resolved and unresolved) in Black America, Native America, Hispanic America, and Asian America. The effort was not meant to create new legislation, but to change the heart. Ambassador Johnson Cook recalls as the group focused on changing mind-sets and the heart, legislation could have been a powerful tool. "Well, it [race] is a heart issue, but legislation helps to right the wrongs. And so you have to have legislation involved in the process. You have to have legislation that levels the playing field, which is why the argument for affirmative action is so profound. Because you can't say that entire groups of people have been left out of the process. Sometimes it's the legislation that drives the heart to change. And it's the situation where finally, I have the opportunity to be with people I would have never been with had not the laws been changed."

During Clinton's second term there were a large number of Black reporters covering the White House, and we were engaged on the race dialogue as reporters and as people of color. There was a strong effort by both sides, the White House and the Black reporters, to have a sit down with President Clinton on the race matter. President Clinton was eager to get there even in the midst of the scandals that were rocking his administration at the time. President Clinton felt it was an important meeting he had to attend for various reasons. Clinton is the only Commander in Chief to ever do that.

I had invited him to a "soul food dinner." Clinton started off saying he was happy to attend because, "Well, you invited me." But it went beyond that. The President revealed more, saying, "You'd be amazed how many times people never invite people once they get to be President to anything on a human scale. I mean you get invited to lots of fund-raisers and dinners. 'Would you come speak at my dinner?' I mean, I'm just talking about go out to dinner and talk. You'd be amazed how little that happens even now with me. It rarely happens. So you giving me a chance to eat food I like with people I like, and have a fun conversation and just go be a person for a night, I loved it. I really liked the food. I really liked you—I don't eat half that stuff anymore, but I did it, because I felt at home doing it. It was something that made me feel like I was home again."

But early on in the race conversation there was a perfect storm that seemed to be on the horizon. The possibility of an apology for slavery for the enslavement of Africans in America looked as if it could have been forthcoming. There was a palpable excitement in the air in certain circles. The time seemed right. However, President Clinton could not have this dialogue without talking about the pain of slavery. And we thought for sure making the historic trip to Africa was setting the stage for this to happen.

Dr. Gardere pondered the question of whether an apology was possible. He said, "Should there be an apology? Absolutely! And I'll tackle this as a psychologist. If you have done something to someone which is very, very wrong, even though at the time you felt that it was part of living, part of history, part of life, now you have evolved and realized it was wrong. By apologizing and giving an acknowledgment to that person, to the victim, that vindicates them. They are then able to say, 'Thank you. Thank you for telling me that you were wrong. And now, I feel better about this because your acknowledging what you did was wrong. I feel better now. I'm able to forgive you.' By apologizing you're able to vindicate yourself from something you draw from and get to your next level of your evolution. Forgiveness is power for the victim and the aggressor. Forgiveness is empowerment. Forgiveness is humanistic. Forgiveness allows you to move on towards a more positive and spiritual cleansing life, for you and the generations to come underneath you."

It was almost as if there was a concerted campaign against a slavery apology. Much like a roller coaster, the conversation on an apology and reparations would quickly pick up steam, only to find another hill around the next corner. According to Mike McCurry, "It was never going to happen." So while he didn't think it would come about, he did point out that my prodding had some effect. "I remember rolling my eyes and more or less dismissing the question of reparations for slavery without learning that there is a deep and emotional chord of response in the Black community on that issue. Your questions forced me to learn more. Not to change position, but to at least speak with a little more sensitivity."

That apology, with any cleansing, was not meant to be. A document dump of emails from the Clinton Presidential Library in March of 2014 shows President Clinton's head speechwriter at the time had the words of an apology in the speech about Goree Island, Senegal. But the words were ultimately removed from the speech and never uttered publicly. Some of the other statements struck from the President's speech were truths, but they did not want them there. One section that was underlined with "no" next to it read "for some of America's ancestors, the journey to America was not the search for the American Dream, it was a nightmare." Another line deleted, "Generation after generation, until my own lifetime, millions upon millions of African Americans worked hard, obeyed the law, built homes and communities. They loved America, but they were not full members of the American Family."

During this "flurry" of race-focused initiatives, there were even plans for a book to be written on the topic in order to help Americans understand this policy of inclusion. As with many prominent projects, a ghostwriter had been retained to help put the President's ideas on the topic into a book. However, we began hearing rumblings around the Press Room that the ghostwriter was somewhat vocal about the project, something that goes against the entire concept of having a ghostwriter. Much like the reparations issue, the "Race Book" idea was eventually scrapped, and the end result was a pamphlet that was created and distributed to Congress.

Those race-based missed opportunities are seen as low points, but there were many accomplishments that dramatically impacted the poor and minority communities. President Clinton, keenly aware of this, makes sure to tout those accomplishments. During the 2014 Civil Rights Summit he told the audience he was able to bring one hundred times more people from poverty to the middle class during his time as President compared to the twelve years prior in the Republican administrations. Clinton is credited with low inflation, lower welfare numbers, and some of the lowest unemployment figures in modern times. Early on in the administration, there was a change to get more done. It was the first time the White House and both houses of Congress were held by the same party.

Tavis Smiley, radio and TV talk show host, pondered Clinton's actions on race and poverty. "Clinton did wonderfully well at appointing Black federal judges. He appointed, as you know, more Black federal judges during his eight years than every President combined prior to him. So in terms of African Americans, given the way we are now, maltreated by the criminal justice system, you know how the justice system treats us. It is a beautiful thing to see. There are a lot of other things, certainly. Appointing people to his administration in positions of power and authority, etc. Clinton did a lot of good."

For the past twenty to thirty years, Bill Clinton is often used as the barometer for both Democrats and Republicans who follow him. Yet even with the good feeling of a strong connection with this White President, for African Americans the White House was still a mystery. Doug Wilder said, "Is the White House still a mystery to African Americans? The answer is 'yes.' I think a better question, 'Has the level of the Clinton years diminished or has it gone up?' If it has diminished, where has the diminishment occurred? Look at the direct cabinet appointments that has gone down. Another question should be why. You don't sacrifice anything by putting people of quality in office, by including people of color, by including people of a different gender. What bothers me, who is calling the ultimate shots in these things? Executive authority, the ultimate shot is your call."

According to Mike McCurry, the administration made a concerted effort. "We put a high premium on outreach and maintaining close relationships with our supporters in the African American community. It was not always smooth sailing, but President Clinton always took the time to talk to and listen to leaders in the community. He was our single best 'Outreach Officer.'"

His outreach was viewed as sincere and effective by both Blacks and Whites. Reverend Jesse Jackson, the man President Clinton has called the architect of his administration's effort to bridge the "Digital Divide," says that Clinton, "from the South," at times a racist region in the nation's history, would "never be seen as pandering." Clinton's feelings about Jackson are mutual, as he said in his Harlem office that Reverend Jackson has always pulled for the poor Black and the poor White person, specifically those in Appalachia.

At least one future White presidential contender openly revealed he wanted to capture the Clinton magic when it came to the Black community. Even in the worst of times for Clinton, especially during the Monica Lewinsky scandal and impeachment, Blacks stood by Clinton because he was "with" Black America. William Jefferson Clinton is a person comfortable in his own skin, no matter the setting. He could stand and sing all three verses of the "Negro National Anthem," something many Blacks cannot do. He has said in the past that he memorized the words because they are moving. He could also sit down for a soul food dinner and eat chitlins like it was caviar (at least before his dietary restrictions).

On March 1, 2004, John Kerry, then a Democratic presidential contender, startled many when he spoke directly about Clinton and race while he was on the campaign trail. There could be no backpedaling on the extreme pander. It occurred at one of Kerry's African American coming-out parties at Morgan State University in Baltimore, Maryland.

Kerry said, "President Clinton was often known as the first Black President. I wouldn't be upset if I could earn the right to be the second." But what exactly was Kerry trying to emulate? Kerry said at the Historically Black Colleges and Universities (HBCU) just an hour and a half away from 1600 Pennsylvania Avenue, "It's a question of keeping faith with the community and doing things that really make a difference."

House Minority Leader James Clyburn was asked about the Kerry statement. "Well, well, that's his feelings. I never bought into the first Black President." I asked Clyburn about the Kerry remarks during the first term of President Barack Obama. He said, "I'm only giving that to Barack Obama."

But what was the tangible difference Kerry mentioned beyond the pander? He wanted a substantial connection to his base. Later his wife, Teresa Heinz Kerry, did acknowledge she was African American, which is true since she was born in Mozambique and eventually became a naturalized citizen of the United States.

As the last months, weeks, and days of the Clinton Administration were winding down, baseball great and humanitarian Hank Aaron boasted of the Clinton years while at the same time fearing the unknown of the incoming forty-third President, saying Blacks were "spoiled" and then bemoaned that he was "scared" of the incoming Bush Administration's expected lack of inclusion. Aaron made the statements to reporters, including to me and the Associated Press's Jesse Holland, in a tent on the South Lawn of the Executive Mansion. He was there being honored for his efforts in breaking the color barrier and for his excellence in Major League Baseball. Just months later, Aaron was back at the White House being celebrated for excellence in baseball by the new President and baseball enthusiast, George W. Bush. Also on hand that day was an elated Negro League player, Buck O'Neil, who gladly signed baseballs for the crowd. Former President Bill Clinton credits George W. Bush with having the most diverse Republican administration. But thus far, Bill Clinton is clearly the reigning champion of all administrations on diversity within the Executive Mansion ranks.

The Black embrace of Clinton started on a national scale with his late friend, confidant, and campaign manager from 1989 to 1993, Democratic Party Chairman, and former Commerce Secretary Ron Brown. Clinton credited Brown for his rise to the White House. Those close to Brown contend he saw potential in Clinton after the beating he survived during his run for President in 1992. Brown believed he had such an awareness of people and what is next. He was like a real visionary. Clinton returned the favor for helping him become President by fulfilling Ron Brown's dream of creating a flourishing trade partnership with Sub-Saharan African democracies, which are in place and were expanded upon by the Bush Administration through the African Growth and Opportunity Act.

Bill Clinton's "Black experience" during his eight years as President included a never-before presidential recognition of Africa with an historic five-nation tour of Sub-Saharan Africa. President Clinton spared no expense in an official visit and celebration for South Africa's first Black President Nelson Mandela in 1994. That was after the United States failed to assist with the efforts to end the brutal racist regimes that kept the lifeblood of apartheid alive in South Africa for years.

Clinton apologized to the elderly Black subjects of the Tuskegee syphilis study. Apologizes were also handed out to Black World War II veterans denied presidential honors because of their color. In addition, Mr. Clinton formed the

"One America" race initiative to help in healing America's racial divide during his second term. Many thought that President Clinton had the right idea. Race is not a partisan issue. It is a social, spiritual issue that has to be dealt with.

However, not every Black person bought into the "honorary title" bestowed on Mr. Clinton. Bob Johnson, founder of Black Entertainment Television and the RLJ Companies, said, "I think the affectionate description of Bill Clinton as the first Black President was based on his absolute camaraderie—simpatico relationships, street talk, however you want to define it—with Black people, both those in his inner circle and in his administration and those folks on the street. That's one. The second is, it has always been said that somehow Black folks from the South and White folks from the South have an understanding even better than White folks and Black folks in the North. They had lived in that same environment where a rural handshake means something . . . and even going all the way back to when Black families helped raise White families. So that type of relationship is sometimes contradictory, but sometimes that connection happens. Then you throw in Bill's natural gregariousness, his comfort at hanging out late at parties, even his comfort at arriving late to a party and staying later than everybody else, his unique ability to be in a room with twenty people and start talking to one person and you get that feeling that there's nobody in the room but you. When you add all of those things together—his style, his emotion, things like he said to a lot of Black folks when we would sing the Black national anthem. One of his favorite lines was 'I'm the only person in the room who knows all of the verses.' And it was absolutely true. It's a lot of truisms in Bill Clinton. So when you take all of those things about how he related to Black people, I don't care whether you were a Black person who was a wealthy intellectual or whether you were just a Black person on the street. It was easy to see President Clinton as 'Bill.' In fact, one of the most difficult things I have with whenever I meet him, I sometimes slip and call him 'Bill,' and forget 'President Clinton.' That's the man. That's why . . . it was officially bestowed with pride by Black people on him as our first Black President."

I was curious about what Johnson thought about the moniker. As an entrepreneur and developer of Black Entertainment Television, he surely has a unique view of the intersection where pop culture and Black culture meet.

He told me, "He so understood, identified, and supported and cared about Black people and Black people had more access to him than any other President of the United States, we were saying we feel about him as part of our family, as someone who cares about us, who is willing to talk to us straight and be authentic with us and not try to patronize us or in some way cater to us. So that's the Bill Clinton that we were talking about."

But what about the rest of his administration? While there was no official apology (much less talk of reparations), the Black community was reaping the benefits of a compassionate President. However, it would take more than that to initiate substantive changes. Mike McCurry commends the forty-second President for his progressive actions. Before Obama arrived on the scene, McCurry wondered if it would actually happen.

"The truth is the White House is a pyramid structure and the juice flows from the top down. And until we have a Black President or Black Vice President or Black Chief of Staff or a Black Deputy Chief of Staff, you really will not see the kind of decision-making authority that you would really need to see to say we have really truly exercised the power within the White House."

Surely there were Black voices at the table, but there were some issues that were not addressed as well as some people had hoped. Tavis Smiley said, "I don't want to overstate it. I think Clinton did an admirable job in a lot of ways. There are things he fell down on. There is no doubt about that. Clinton also had a lot of things that disappointed a whole lot of us. Moving too slow to go into Rwanda during the genocides there, sitting on his hands too long." (Interestingly enough, that is a regret Clinton wrote about in his post-presidency.) Smiley also said, "I was not fond of the Welfare Bill. As you recall, Marion Wright Edelman's husband, Peter Edelman, quit the Clinton Administration in protest over that welfare bill. I hated his crime bill that put into effect 100-to-1 crack powder cocaine discrepancy that became the law of the land."

Even though Clinton touts some of the lowest welfare roll numbers during his time in office, again White House staffers were deeply divided on the issue of making the welfare bill law. The legislation the President signed into law in 1996 cut spending over a six-year period by $54 billion. The President's action also transferred control over the welfare program from the federal government to the states. Critics say Clinton's signature on the paper ended the sixty-year guarantee of assistance for eligible, poor Americans. In later years to spin the issue as a service to people and the nation, the White House began employing individuals who had previously been on the welfare program. They never provided names, but they made sure we were aware that it was meant as an incentive for others and to demonstrate welfare reform was working.

As Smiley looks back and gives a measured ranking for Clinton's work in the Black community, he said, "In the years to come, as more and more is written about the Clinton years, I think we're going to see he was on balance as a President. But Clinton did not do everything right."

Throughout my meeting with him on that snowy January day, and to his credit, Clinton seemed eager to expound on his accomplishments and his drawbacks. In true political fashion, he started off with his successes. "You know I did a good job with appointments. I did a good job with considering race. We had fabulous results economically, but my biggest disappointments were not being able to crack the criminal justice disparity and to close the remaining economic, education, and health care gaps. I thought if we can make this much progress, we ought to be able to eliminate them altogether. And with the benefit of history and seeing, for example, President Obama dealing with the fact that a part of Congress doesn't want to ratify any of his economic policies. He's dealing with the fact that it typically takes ten years for any country to get over a financial collapse. We had two in the nineteenth century in America—1873 and 1893. It wasn't just recession, it was the financial systems. Both of them took about ten years before normal growth resumed. I'd been thinking all along, 'What can we do to speed this up? We gotta speed this up.' Maybe there's nothing I could've done, but I sure had a good time trying."

President Clinton certainly racked up some Black points on the side of the minority farmer, as he said to me while gazing out of the window onto 125th Street. "I've tried to help rural America. In rural farming states that were overwhelming Republican, did real well when I was President."

That's true. He did help a group of farmers correct an injustice at the hands of the USDA with the *Pigford* lawsuit. However, the financial harvest did not come to fruition until about two decades later during the first term of President Barack Obama. John Boyd said, "Eighty thousand Black farmers missed the deadline to participate in the class action lawsuit. The Office of Civil Rights at USDA was closed during the Reagan Administration. The Black farmers' complaints were found with years of dust on them and 'never processed.' Over twenty-two thousand Black farmers petitioned to get into the class action on time. Only fourteen thousand were meritorious and received $50,000, and nine thousand were denied compensation due to the fact we had to find a similarly situated White farmer to compare our case to. The Black farmer settlement is still the largest settlement in history for Black America."

In 1984 the complaint was filed against the USDA, but during the Clinton years Boyd would walk Pennsylvania Avenue with a mule called Struggle to dramatize the plight of the farmers who were hurting. Boyd said, "At the turn of the century there were over one million Black farmers in the United States who tilled over twenty million acres of land. Today, a little over thirty thousand Black farmers own less than three million acres. A foodless culture will surely starve to death and perish."

To possibly shed a light on what would happen if the subject of true reparations for Black Americans was actually explored and examined, I was curious to find out what the farmers actually had to go through, despite the small amount that most received. Boyd remembered chronologically what it took to begin the process to get restitution. He recalled that "in 1994, I began protesting against the USDA's discrimination of Black farmers by using the familiar 'forty acres and a mule' slogan to bring attention to the plight of the Black farmer. In 1997, we filed the Black farmers' lawsuit. I met with then-President Bill Clinton who settled the case. The Department of Agriculture with its ugly, racist head filed motions in federal court to deny the Black farmers class notification! The USDA did not come forward with the names and addresses of the farmers who filed complaints." Eventually the case dragged on through two other presidencies before the restitution conclusion. Unfortunately, over that time many of those who initially filed had transitioned this life, but a wrong was made right.

So while the Clinton Administration was one of progress for Blacks and other minorities, that didn't mean everyone at the White House was on board. Others who worked in the administration and even in the media didn't necessarily agree with the policies, and of course being a Black reporter on the scene, I witnessed plenty of that. I'm all for respecting the Office of the President, and I know that there are traditions to follow, but for some reason every time Clinton came into the room, "Hail to the Chief" would be blasting to signal his arrival. That's fine, but it became almost a joke it was done so much. When I voiced my opinion that I thought it was overkill, a fellow reporter quickly suggested that I was "unpatriotic." I don't know if that lashing out was due to the atmosphere at the time, but I didn't let it bother me. I have a tough skin. Trust me, I've been called worse. I still have a job to do.

So I was curious what Clinton thought about what it would be like going forward. Would there be any movement on Black issues with future administrations? When you look back at his time in office, his policies did affect Blacks more so than any other time in recent history. Former President Clinton said of the future for Blacks in this county, "I think African Americans cannot close these remaining gaps until we have a better overall economic policy. But I also think and hope that we will see a lot of attention devoted to things that will really help people succeed at home and at work. I spent a lot of time with helping people succeed at home and at work with the Family Leave Law. Welfare reform had a lot more money for childcare and for transportation and other things. We need to go back to that. We can't have people making policy just on who's voting for them." I think he's right. It might be a lofty goal in this time of partisan politics, but elected officials, especially Presidents, can't just serve those who gave them a vote. They have a duty to everyone.

History has been and always will be the judge of Presidents and how their decisions impacted the country. As far as Bill Clinton, there many positive and negative aspects to his time in office. There's no denying that. But on matters of race, I believe William Jefferson Clinton definitely helped to push the ball forward, unfortunately not enough, but he did a significant amount of work that is still apparent years later. I think Ernie Green has the best explanation of the eight years from January 1993 to January 2001.

Ernie Green is a historic figure in his own right. He is a member of the Little Rock Nine, a group of Black children who integrated Little Rock Central High School, drawing the ire of racists in this nation. However, Green and Clinton did not meet until Clinton was Attorney General of Arkansas. Green was also a part of the Carter Administration in the Labor Department as Assistant Secretary. Green says of Clinton: "You finally have to get the rest of the country to see Black people as full participants, full players able to be competitive. And, to me, that is probably Clinton's greatest contributing legacy. You can argue all that you want to about what he did or didn't do. No American President has forced the country to see Black folks as people [the way he did]."

Ironically, the last day for President Clinton in the Oval Office fell on Martin Luther King Day. It was January 20, 2001. Clinton reflected on that day. "When I left office, my last message was on Martin Luther King Day, the last day I served as President, and I pointed out the continuing disparities in American life, the disparities and poverty rate and per capita income and employment rate and college graduation rate in the criminal justice system. I am especially disappointed that we were not able to make more progress there."

PRESIDENT BUSH

Higgh drama ushered in the George W. Bush Administration, and the newsworthy thrills remained constant for most of his eight years in office. The government scenes played out on the world stage covering various topics and issues, and matters of color were included. The spectacle began in the political fight over who would become the nation's forty-third President, with Al Gore chasing what he thought was his and then–Texas Governor George W. Bush staking claim to the title of Commander in Chief at the same time. To say the nation was divided could be considered the ultimate understatement. As a White House journalist, I had a bird's-eye view of the political firestorm that was brewing.

That November 2000 night, the Nashville press filing center was jammed with reporters waiting to pen quotes from either a victory or a concession speech. Instead, we pulled an all-nighter, waiting for Al Gore's decision not to go down without a fight. It was an office he had been groomed for since childhood, following in his father, Senator Al Gore Sr.'s, footsteps in the family business. Politics.

Suddenly, a loud scream went out over the spacious, overcrowded room. Gore aide and supporter Anne Edwards elatedly said, "Did I hear it right? They called Florida for Gore?" This was one of those news stories where the "facts" seemed to keep changing. We would get a tip that would later be contradicted by another, supposedly more reliable tip. It was chaos as everyone realized that the country's direction would be affected by this outcome, one that seemed to be teetering indefinitely.

Later that evening, unsure of the time, we worked to get news on Al Gore's thoughts in the midst of the news frenzy. Change happened at breakneck speed. A pall fell over the Gore Nashville campaign headquarters camp like a drawn shade. ABC News took the state of Florida, a huge political "get," out of the Gore win column. The wound was swift and fatal. That night was the beginning of weeks of questions about the election and confusion over the forty-third presidency of this country. We now know the outcome. It was not a textbook finish by any means, but it is certainly something for the annals of history. "W" got it.

Secretary of State Colin Powell, one of the few African Americans with a presidential pedigree who was once thought of as presidential material, contends, "You gotta win an election, and I don't say that flippantly." For weeks the nation was divided and held in limbo as we pondered, How did we end up in a "tie"? Why wasn't there a clear winner? What exactly does it take to reach the highest office? Powell's winning formula: "You have a combination of intelligence, character and synchronization with the thinking of the American people at the time that you are running for office. A synchronization where you can capture their hopes and their fears and their ambitions and their dreams and become one of them and one with them so that they will elect you. If you can do that, you're going to be President. If you don't do that, you're not going to be President." Powell used the fortieth President as an example. "Reagan did it very well during my time in the White House, and people have said, 'Well, he wasn't very detailed, he didn't pay attention to things, he might have been slowing down a little bit.' All might be true and all is certainly arguable, but what is not arguable is that he did all the things I just said. He projected an image to the American people. He had goals that they understood. But more than understanding, they shared—they were their goals as well as his goals. And he personified what they wanted to see in their leadership and that's why he became President even if he wasn't a master of details."

In 2000 the Supreme Court and Florida's labored recount of "dimpled" and "pregnant" chads eventually determined the Oval Office outcome. Of course, the Black vote was included among those who helped determine the election results. George W. Bush and his team knew their base and did not focus a lot of energy on trying to win over the Black vote, ultimately gaining only 8 percent of the African American tally, a small drop down from Ronald Reagan's numbers.

So once he was anointed to the ultimate office, George W. Bush instantly had the weight of the world on his shoulders. Former President Bill Clinton agreed. "Yeah, his biggest problem was when he got elected." From the very beginning, expectations of President George W. Bush and his administration to carry over the concerted engagement with Black America from the previous administration were predictably low, but of course as a reporter I wanted to find out for myself. At 10:30 a.m. on May 31, 2001, at the Roosevelt Room of the White House, I had my first opportunity to get a glimpse into the person who had recently moved into the White House. Due to a no-show, I was given the distinction of sitting front and center as the forty-third President of the United States, George W. Bush, conducted one of his first meetings with the media.

It was a stroke of luck because of course as reporters we always want face time with a sitting President . . . on the record. If we are not allowed that opportunity, any time with him gives us a chance to question him directly and report on his responses. So that day I was told to move one seat over, positioned at the distinguished wooden table, directly across from, and face to face with, this new Republican President. The meeting of about nine radio correspondents was classified as a "get to know you" session. Each President typically holds some sort of off-the-record session with reporters who cover him full time at the White House. But the real focus took place after the round-table discussion when there was a free-flowing conversation at the end of the event. A relaxed and more provocative question-and-answer session began covering religion, Ivy Leaguers, and race just before he was to leave.

To my surprise, President Bush came across as approachable and relatable as he shared with us that he didn't particularly care much for those with Ivy League degrees. Of course, we all perked up since he had graduated from Yale University, albeit with a "C" average. It was my opinion that if he had displayed more of this person while on the campaign trail, he would have likely won a larger percentage of the African American vote. I was not making that statement in support of his presidential victory over Al Gore, but observing as a journalist who is skilled at measuring the reaction of the Black community to various presidential occurrences.

Bush received similar numbers from the African American community during the presidential election as did when he ran for the Texas governor's seat against the late Ann Richards. In that election he received 9 percent of the Black vote. Unexpectedly, President Bush also revealed his own theory as to why he did not gain the Black vote. He gave a litany of reasons, saying because "I am Republican, I was a Governor of Texas, and my stand on the death penalty." I interrupted saying, "Blacks often consider the state racist." He quickly followed with, "Yes!" This question still begged for an answer: How could a man who did not gain the Black vote, which proved important and even pivotal during the prior two presidential elections, ultimately win the Oval Office?

I turned to one who should know when I posed that question to Bill Clinton. "Like I said, I consider him my friend. I think his economic policies were wrong, but people would listen to him because they could sense that he didn't have a racist bone in his body and his father certainly didn't either. He, then-Connecticut Senator George H. W. Bush, voted for open housing in 1968. There weren't many Southern Republicans around doing that. They thought that they were going to become a majority party in the South because the Democrats had supported all the civil rights and in many places, that turned out to be true, but he just thought it was the right thing to do, and he did it."

As a reporter, it's my job to get as many opinions as possible. So I did my best to schedule an interview for this book with former President George W. Bush. I hoped that he would elaborate on his policies and other comments. After many attempts to speak with him, Freddy Ford, Communications Director and Personal Aide to George W. Bush, wrote in an e-mail: "I'm sorry to say that unfortunately we have to respectfully decline the offer to be interviewed for the book. As you know, President Bush is pretty happy to be out of the limelight these days and as a matter of policy he just doesn't give many interviews or participate in book projects. I hope you understand. Having said that, I want you to know that he smiled when he heard your name and asked me to thank you for thinking of him. He was really happy to have heard from you and wishes you well on the project." The irony is the Bush office ultimately declined participation in my project the day of the Civil Rights Summit at the LBJ Library in Texas.

Bill Clinton had something to add about his predecessor's administration's record on race. "A majority of the conservatives in the Republican Party decided that President Bush's politics on inclusion were a loss for them and they could do better, by taking a tough line. In effect, keep the vote down, not just among African Americans and Hispanics, but also among students and people with disabilities and lower income, and older White voters who tend to vote Democrat. And they had two great examples of what happens when people only want to vote for President." Clinton remembered that Bush won the election with "40 percent of the Hispanic vote" and "the point is he got people to listen to him."

But the 2000 minority vote for former Democratic Vice President Al Gore was high. Gore received 95 percent of the Black vote in 2000, just a few percentage points higher than John Kerry in 2004 according to Gallup polling. Gore was the heir apparent. It was seen as his race to lose as Blacks were heeding his call to stick with him for a continuation of prosperity. But Gore lost. He could not win his home state of Tennessee, a Bible Belt state where many residents did not like his pro-choice stance. Also, a major problem is that Gore did not take advantage of the connection to one of the most popular Presidents in modern times. Americans were coming off an eight-year love affair with Bill Clinton, and they were learning to like Gore simply because of the connection. It just wasn't the same. The silence of not hearing the accomplishments from the Clinton-Gore Administration was deafening. Gore chose to leave those achievements out, in large part because of the Lewinsky scandal. That was a politically fatal mistake.

After weeks of wondering who would take the White House for at least the next four years after President Clinton, the U.S. Supreme Court stepped in and declared presidential victory for George W. Bush by upholding the Florida vote count. It ultimately came down to dimpled and pregnant chads in the state where Bush's brother, Jeb, was Governor. It was not a textbook race by any means, but certainly one for the annals of history. The very act of voting was the deciding factor—the electoral college votes were in George W. Bush's favor.

From 2001 to 2009, there were a plethora of newsworthy events for us reporters to cover during the issue-plagued administration. From the beginning there were low expectations of this President. But he keenly knew that whatever he did would draw the ire of some. For others he would easily surpass their marginal expectations. So he charted his own course, not worrying about his naysayers. His first year in office saw unimaginable tragedy and resilience after 9/11. Soon after the worst attack on American soil, the United States fought terrorism in Afghanistan and invaded Iraq, eventually bring down Saddam Hussein and his alleged efforts to supply terrorists with weapons of mass destruction that were never found.

But in the lead up to the Iraq War, White House reporters struggled to get a glimpse inside the Bush mind-set on this possible U.S. military campaign. Eventually the President revealed his heart during the March 6, 2003, night-time press conference. I wanted, like any other reporter, to find out what he was thinking at this time of crisis and inevitable war. So I asked about his thoughts on the Congressional Black Caucus's call for diplomacy when it came to war, and I also asked, "How is your faith guiding you?" He responded first by talking about the groups supporting diplomatic means to end the Iraq stalemate. Within that two-minute-and-eighteen-second response, he exposed a side the public rarely saw. He showed his heart when he answered my question on his faith by saying, "My faith sustains me because I pray daily. I pray for guidance and wisdom and strength. If we were to commit our troops—if we were to commit our troops, I would pray for their safety and I would pray for the safety of innocent Iraqi lives, as well."

The emotion at this point was undeniable as tears welled up in his eyes. I did not understand immediately what was happening as I watched our President getting emotional as cameras clicked behind me to capture that rare, genuine moment of a red-faced, teary-eyed President. George W. Bush told me, "One thing that is

: about our country, April, is there are thousands of people who pray for me that I will never be able to thank. But it is a humbling experience to think that people I will never have met have lifted me and my family up in prayer. And for that I am grateful. It's been a comforting feeling to know that is true. I would pray for their safety. I pray for peace, April! I pray for peace."

I took a lot of heat for that question, particularly from the Black community. However, that's part of my job. I have to assess the situation and decide what I think is the appropriate question, one that will elicit the best response for my audience. I remember talking to my friend and former Baltimore City Mayor Kurt Schmoke. We emailed back and forth about my question and Bush's response. Schmoke's email stated, "April, It was a good question, but I think I understand why you are catching grief. For some reason, with one or two exceptions, the entire tone of the last press conference seemed more like a seminar and less like the usual give and take of press conferences. There seemed a noticeable lack of confrontation in the tone of the questions, which was surprising from a Press Corps that understands how deeply divided the country is about the war. I think many of your fans wanted to hear you reflect the anxieties prevalent, particularly in the Black community, about the current situation. Unfortunately, the subtle brilliance of your question was probably lost among those who heard one reporter ask about an analogy to Vietnam and among those of an older era who remember Dan Rather confronting Nixon in a press conference about Watergate matters. Don't fret and keep being yourself. Personal integrity is crucial in your business, so you shouldn't start asking questions only driven by 'polls,' Cheers, Kurt."

Soon after that press conference, the United States, along with other nations, invaded Iraq. At the White House, you could feel the mood before things happened, very serious with an eerie quiet. I was in an interview with advisor Karen Hughes, and that interview was cut short in her office as she had to run to President Bush's office. It was different from other meetings cut short. It was March 20, 2003, the day the war began. The fight against terrorism began depleting the financial surplus William Jefferson Clinton had amassed before leaving office. The nation found itself needing money and going to China and Switzerland for help to fund the war and to keep our economy going. Times were getting rough economically, and minorities especially were feeling the pinch more now than before, even with the current Republican economic structure. People were in shock and notably agitated, never a good combination. In addition, the Congressional Black Caucus was very vocal about their opinion that this was not the time to go to war. One reason: there would be a disproportionate number of Black soldiers on the front lines.

Bush economics did come into play on the race front. Bill Clinton, a fierce political competitor and now a protective friend of former President George W. Bush, said, "Unlike his father [George Herbert Walker Bush] actually believed in trickle-down economics that Ronald Reagan practiced in. So that's why it's a doubling of the debt. Not that many jobs out there. I think he's wrong about that, but they also believed in empowerment."

Mary Frances Berry, former Head of the U.S. Commission on Civil Rights, said of the George W. Bush White House, "As far as policy was concerned, his policy was awful. The Justice Department, Civil Rights division has been documented by hearings in the Congress and by media accounts. He was running the Voting Rights Section and he had not one case of discrimination against Blacks, the whole time they [the Bush Administration] were there." In addition, "the Justice Department was terrible" because on the voting rights issue the Bush Justice Department found "they [Black people] were interfering with White people with voting." But Bill Clinton countered, saying, "Remember George Bush said his best phrase is that 'we shouldn't give in to the soft bigotry of low expectations' and I think he believed that."

But as these policies were made, who was in his ear who was Black and aware of all sides of the cultural spectrum? Berry believes, "Black Republicans do what Black Democrats do. If you want to be in an administration, and you want a political job, then you have to play the political game. So whatever they're playing, they are partisan for whatever the party is trying to do."

While General Colin Powell, revered and regarded, was the voice of reason at times, President Bush's innermost circle also included someone who lived through and was impacted by deadly racism in the South in the 1960s. Berry said, "In terms of Bush, Condi Rice had a close relationship with Bush. And in order to have a close relationship with Bush, there were certain opinions you must have." Berry goes on to say, "I think it's healthy to have Black folks in both parties. I just think some of the policies that parties follow are not good for Black folks."

African American Housing and Urban Development Secretary Alphonso Jackson says it was more than creating a picture for President Bush who "put them in positions where you can't in any way contest their abilities. You can't contest Colin's ability. Colin was the chief architect for our foreign policy. You can't contest Condi's ability." Clinton, the President with the most diverse administration to date, remarked that George W. Bush had the most diverse Republican administration ever and there was a very special relationship forged with Condi Rice and President George W. Bush. Clinton said, "You know he had a lot of African Americans in the administration. He probably trusted Condi al security more than anything else and he believed that we ought

Following 9/11 and the war, Bush was faced with another domestic challenge. The needs in New Orleans were dire after the wrath of Hurricane Katrina. The Department of Energy approved a request for a loan of six million barrels of crude oil from the Strategic Petroleum Reserve (SPR) to prevent any potential supply disruptions as a result of the hurricane. The oil was released in an agreement between the Energy Department and ExxonMobil. The amount was larger than the 5.4 million barrel loans during Hurricane Ivan in September 2004. That release marked the seventh time that has ever happened under an exchange agreement.

Dr. Jeff Gardere said, "Even if he had very conservative policies or felt that there was no such thing or that the racism is being overplayed and he felt that there was real equality and so on, if he had tried more would we have seen that he does more with Africa and so on? I think a lot more people would have respected him—people of color or many more liberals. I mean, let's not forget two of the most influential people in his inner circle were Colin Powell and Condoleezza Rice. To me, that spoke volumes, for you to have those two people in your inner circle and to have those very close relationships, that's where the rubber hits the road. You can talk about all of the liberal agenda you have and how you believe in equality and so on. Unless you're showing it to me, unless I see it in your relationships, then to me, that's empty talk. That's empty talk. And with Colin Powell and Condoleezza Rice, I think he showed a real connection that was . . . a true mirror into his soul . . . as to what he thought about people . . . especially people of color, that he would put them in those extremely high positions and trusted them."

Another challenge when a new administration comes in is that there's a new Press Secretary, and I have to work to establish a productive relationship. The White House Briefing Room is a dicey deal as the cameras can bring added pressure as the world is literally watching and scrutinizing each syllable delivered. It is also a room where sometimes the unintended words or "mis-speaks" are magnified. One of those times was the highly anticipated first day on the job of late Press Secretary Tony Snow. Snow was quite a character in every sense of the word.

It was standing room only in the Briefing Room that day, and I even had to stand on the side wall as I could not get to my seat. Someone had commandeered my spot! But I had a great vantage point with an unobstructed view over the seated crowd. Tony visibly relished the moment. It was about the news emanating out of the White House, but it was also about the conservative broadcaster's new job. He made news that day when he was answering questions, specifically when ABC White House Correspondent Martha Raddatz, who has been in the war zone of Iraq and Afghanistan, did not get an answer to her question. In his long, drawn-out response as to why not to declass the President's surveillance program, Tony gave words that racist past that kids can read about in the story of Brer Rabb his first day, responded by saying, "I don't want to hug the tar baby of trying to comment on the program . . . I could neither confirm nor deny."

After he made that comment and I audibly gasped, a seasoned White reporter turned around and told me to "shut up, you tar baby." I went to Tony Snow's office and told him the words he used were wrong, and I informed him of the incident that followed. He apologized immediately, saying he did not mean it that way and was not thinking, but of course the media grabbed hold. The reporter who made the rude comment to me was confronted by Mark Smith of the White House Correspondents' Association and later by his Latina wife. I received an email on May 16, 2006, from the reporter stating he was "penitent." The damage was done, but I did what Blacks do every day and have done for decades—I forgave, and we all had to move on. But it left a scar. Incidents like that always do.

The nation's second Black Secretary of State, Condi Rice, is the daughter of two Republican African American teachers. The Rice family did not conform to the standards of the day. Her father, John Wesley Rice, was angry about racism and did not follow the edict of Dr. King of meeting racial violence with nonviolence. He was ready to meet a violent exchange with his gun, representing some of the philosophies of some other rights leaders of that time. For Secretary Rice, race mattered in the George W. Bush Administration, recalling, "I don't look at the United States through rose-colored glasses. My father couldn't vote back in 1952. I couldn't go to a restaurant until 1964. And so, I could say that America hadn't been perfect in this regard, and I understood that in a very personal way. But it was a good thing to get going to the journey for democracy. So I actually thought it was helpful to be Black and to be able to make that case. And then finally, I was very much an advocate and I think I was known in many places for trying to promote the rights of the African Diaspora population in Brazil and in Colombia. I'll never forget when President Uribe, the Colombian President, appointed his first Black Minister. He actually called me to tell me what he was doing. So, maybe it mattered in that way."

For this book, I was able to talk with former Secretary Rice by phone while she was in her Stanford University office. The conversation immediately took me back to her time at the White House. I thought about how I had conducted my first interview with her as National Security Advisor in her West Wing office where she showed me the portraits that dotted the walls. They had been donated by the Smithsonian. Small plaques below the paintings identified the title and artist. Secretary Rice is an avid football fan, as evidenced by the Cleveland

Browns helmets proudly on display. I always like to investigate a subject's office if I can because it often tells a lot about them. Since I'm from Baltimore, we had an instant friendly rivalry as far as football was concerned. I have spoken to her often since that initial interview, and I am always intrigued by her opinions as a proud African American woman in Bush's inner circle.

Secretary Rice, a supporter of "targets of opportunity" [affirmative action] and a believer in a woman's right to choose, is a darling in the Republican Party although she deviates from their core values at times as she is the sum of her life experiences. She felt the impact of racism in the South, as she was friends with one of the four little girls killed in the bombing of the 16th Street Baptist Church in Birmingham, Alabama. Rice's friend, eleven-year-old Denise McNair, died in the blast that Sunday morning, September 15, 1963. Rice came into the Bush Administration's inner circle with strong ties to the President of the United States, who referred to her as "mother hen."

She acknowledges, "I was his closet advisor and everyone knew that. I do think he brought me into some discussions of some issues because I was Black and female. For instance, Title IX [of the 1972 Education Amendments]. There was a time when people were trying to get us to revise Title IX and I helped him think through that. Because as a woman and also Provost of Stanford and having dealt with issues and Title IX and women's equity issues, I think he felt I had a special perch for that. I was pretty involved in issues of affirmative action. It's documented and it's in my book, actually, about the *Michigan* case and the fact that he brought me into the discussions about whether or not to join the Amicus brief for the *Michigan* case and whether or not to recommend the overturning of *Bakke*. I feel personally that I had an effect on him and the administration's position to let *Bakke* stand in the brief."

In the midst of the revelation above the fold in the major papers, it was revealed that she helped the President determine his stand on his amicus brief against preferences in admissions at the University of Michigan. Many considered it an outrage that she, a Black woman, did that. But Rice went against the majority opinion and that was not originally reported. The morning the news was released, I was in the doctor's office in Baltimore waiting for my annual exam. I received a call from Press Secretary Ari Fleischer, who was riding in like the cavalry extending a lifeline to Rice. He asked me to interview her, and I did a few hours later. It was an attempt by the administration to do some damage control and to get her story out there as soon as possible. It worked. Condi talked about her thoughts on "targets of opportunity" that are needed on occasion. Once her statements were aired, folks, particularly Blacks, were saying that was code for affirmative action and condemning her for just saying those words.

Ironically, the first Black Secretary of State, Colin Powell, is a supporter of affirmative action as the U.S. military was one of the first organizations to integrate but still has challenges with promoting minorities to the upper ranks.

President Bush went against the idea of preferences for admissions to the University of Michigan. That school had quotas to meet for admission, based on race, among other considerations. It seemed a contradiction since President George W. Bush had attended Yale, as did his father, George H. W. Bush. They were a legacy. For many schools in this nation, a family legacy at a school offers more points for admission acceptance. But the big issue was the racial preference piece. President Bush did not feel racial preferences should be allowed. He followed suit with his party's stance against affirmative action.

Dr. Gardere commented, "I don't think President Bush ever hated or ever saw Black people as being less than. I think it goes back to what we talked about, where you feel that color is not really an issue or has to be paid attention to or needs special circumstances. There are a lot of people who feel like there should be no more affirmative action. Those are the people that may not be hateful towards Black people." Gardere has found that people who feel this way have a justification for this attitude. They feel, "There is no real prejudice. We've gone beyond that. We don't need special consideration for very talented Black people who didn't have a lot of the advantages or in fact had many disadvantages, of poverty, of being affected with self-esteem because of race and prejudice and many of those issues."

Yet Rice firmly feels her presence made a difference on race, saying, "One other thing that might interest you, April. You know the fortieth anniversary, the 1964 Civil Rights Act, was in 2004. It's a so-called Public Accommodations Act, so an act that did desegregate restaurants like in Birmingham. We used to have a scheduling meeting for the President, and it was Andy Card, Karl Rove, Karen Hughes, and you know the main senior staff would get together, maybe about seven or eight of us. And on this particular day, there was a question [about whether] the President ought to do an event to commemorate the 2004 Civil Rights Act, or as more people thought we'll just wait and commemorate the Voting Rights Act which is a year later."

Then National Security Advisor Condi Rice "surprised" herself by her reaction, saying, "I was like, you have to understand that this is the act that made it possible for my parents and me to be able to go to a restaurant or a movie theater and this mattered. The memory kind of makes me a little bit stunned."

Even if race was not on the front burners as in some prior administrations, race still was ever present and in some instances the elephant in the room. Rice laughingly remembers, "We had an event. I suggested that we invite, and we

ohnson's daughters because he had indeed been the President
had passed and been largely responsible for getting it through.
t that I could be involved in that way. In terms of being abroad, I
felt that it was an advantage to be able to talk about America from the perspective of someone whose ancestors, even as a little girl—me, but certainly my parents—had not been afforded the benefits of American democracy. Because we were trying to promote democracy and sometimes when we did that, people would bristle a little bit. America was telling them what to do or these were Western values. I could always say, 'I don't look at the United States through rose-colored glasses. My father couldn't vote back in 1952. I couldn't go to a restaurant until 1964.' And so, by no means, I could say that America hadn't been perfect in this regard, and I understood that in a very personal way. But it was a good thing to get going to the journey for democracy, so I actually thought it was helpful to be Black and to be able to make that case."

Like Secretary Rice, the wisdom of women and their "heart" helped guide and fulfill some of President Bush's agenda items. Former First Lady Laura Bush was vigilant on the President's efforts in reducing the numbers of HIV/AIDS infections globally and even in the United States. First Lady Laura Bush traveled the world and even in her own backyard (at the time) of Washington, D.C., to Howard University Hospital to watch the clinical work to reduce and prevent the number of HIV/AIDS infections. On that topic, President Bush has a title that might surprise some. He is known as the President who did more for Africa than any other President. Reverend Jesse Jackson, a critic of the Bush Administration, said, "He [President Bush] was more comfortable giving aid to Africa and the HIV/AIDS crisis, and it made an impact. For many, he will be remembered for that."

Actually, the effort was intense as the White House put people on the ground in Africa to figure out ways to help in curing and preventing the spread of HIV/AIDS to include mother-to-child transmission. There was also an effort to reduce the spread of Malaria and Tuberculosis on the continent. At that time, there was a back and forth in Washington among Republicans about how to help with the health and humanitarian crisis, specifically in Sub-Saharan Africa. Africa was increasingly becoming the hot issue.

In 2005 the Glen Eagles G-8 Summit hosted by then–British Prime Minister Tony Blair focused world leaders on the plight of the darker continent. To this day there are questions about whether all of the pledged funds from that initiative actually made it to Africa. But in Washington, the conversations within the Republican Party were happening. The overriding question was how to help and by how much. The pressure was mounting.

Secretary of State Colin Powell even began framing the discuss the Sub-Saharan Africa HIV/AIDS epidemic a national security crisis. Tony Fratto, Bush's deputy White House Press Secretary, said President Bush had two thoughts on help for Africa. "You have a responsibility to do more if you have more" particularly as "most of the poorest people in the world live in Africa." The concern within the Washington Republican circles was that funding could be wasted if it did not meet the intended goals. Fratto remembers the President felt the money needed to be "effective" and did not feel "that money being wasted was a necessary outcome." President Bush established the Millennium Challenge Corporation (a foreign aid agency), expanded the African Growth and Opportunity Act (AGOA), launched the President's Malaria Initiative (PMI), and established the President's Emergency Plan for AIDS Relief (PEPFAR).

President Bush did not publicly frame Africa's AIDS crisis as a national security issue, but fast forwarding six years later, Mrs. Bush did during our conversation at the 2014 U.S./Africa Summit. She called it both a "moral" and "national security" issue. With firsthand understanding and a deep concern, Mrs. Bush said, "I would say definitely a moral issue. And that's what George thought when he launched PEPFAR. He knew that we were the wealthiest country in the world and he thought if the wealthiest country in the world turned their backs and acted like we didn't care that Africa was going to be a continent of orphans . . . that that was just wrong. It was wrong morally for us as Americans. And so besides being a national security issue, it was also a moral issue to go in and do what we could do. And when we did, when we gave that first money to the global fund for AIDS, other counties followed. And when we went in with PEPFAR, other countries followed."

Clinton noted, "The PEPFAR program was a great program. He was able to get the votes for it because it started at the end of my second term. The Republicans wouldn't have voted for PEPFAR if I proposed it. It was easier for him, and the Democrats would have voted for it under anybody because they believed in it. But the other thing that happened, and I think you got to give a lot of credit to these Christian Evangelicals, they thought of themselves as conservative, but they felt they read the whole Bible. They thought they had a moral obligation to the poor."

But the effectiveness of PEPFAR and the drugs used to combat the diseases did not come until the funeral of Pope John Paul II in 2005. Clinton said, "He [President Bush] invited me to go to the pope's funeral with him, Pope John Paul. So we're riding over there and he says, 'Tell me about your AIDS work.' I started telling him when I started these generic drugs were $500 per person a year an that's a lot less than the $10,000 we pay at the clinic here in Harlem on Medicaid. But it's still a lot of money in a country where the per capita income is less than a dollar a day, and he said, 'Yeah,' and all the drug companies supported President Bush. They were basically more Republican than Democrat, partly because at the end of my term I said we weren't going to enforce patents in life-saving medicines. We had to make some exceptions for international emergency epidemics like AIDS. So he says, 'They tell me these drugs are no good.'"

So basically Clinton offered to help expedite the approval of generics by the Food and Drug Administration (FDA) to provide to Africa in an effort to reduce the high costs of the drug companies, costs that made the program prohibitive otherwise. So in a nonpublicized partnership, Bill Clinton was able to get the generic equivalents for twenty-two drugs approved by the FDA. By the time President Bush left office, a little more than half of the PEPFAR money was used to buy these generic drugs. Thus, American money was responsible for treating 1.7 million people through the PEPFAR program out of a total at that time of about 3.5 million.

Clinton added, "Fast-forward. President Obama became President and asked Hillary to be Secretary of State. PEPFAR is under the State Department because it's international. She found a wonderful African American named Eric Goosby—who had once run one of the first AIDS clinics anywhere, in San Francisco, and later our operation in China—so she appointed him head of PEPFAR. They took the purchases of drugs, you know from 52 to 98 plus percent so that . . . we'd gone from 3.17 million to 5.1 million people. Triple. Three times as many, out of a total population of the world of approximately ten million, maybe eleven million. And they're actually spending slightly less tax-payer money, buying medicine for $5.1 million and making it for $1.7. That's how much difference it makes. So that's what you want. Like when you asked me about disappointments, what you want is for history to emulate MLK's image that the arc of history is long but it bends towards justice. You want to keep things going in the right direction and we did that, I think. Our country's played an honorable role, now under President Bush, President Obama, with lots of help from the Gates foundation, and the work that I do and others around the world kicking in their money. But you don't see that in economics and our economic policy. Our social policies at home are too ridden by ideological differences and too immune from what I would call 'evidence-based decision

George Bush wanted to save people's lives. He just looked at he said, 'If you can prove that these are good drugs, we'll buy o get back to that in America, without regard to party. We've evidence, what works."

Fratto looks back on the Bush Africa Initiative, saying there is "durability" over the years when "you can actually count lives being saved. If it were not for PEPFAR and the Global Fund, 2.5 million people would be dead. That is a pretty powerful thing to be remembered for."

Fratto is right that it is something great to remember, but the legacy continues. Since leaving office in January 2009, former President George W. Bush and former First Lady Laura Bush have been "refurbishing clinics" since they left the Beltway. On August 6, 2014, at the U.S./Africa Summit convened by President Obama, former First Lady Laura Bush attended the event, and during an exclusive interview she said, "One of the things that we learned when we got home was that people who—women who were living with AIDS now because they were on ARVs [antiretroviral drug therapies] were dying with cervical cancer. Cervical cancer is the leading cause of cancer death among women in Africa."

"And cervical cancer is preventable. Very few Americans ever develop cervical cancer because a pap smear is a common part of every woman's physical, but of course that was not the case in Africa. Cervical cancer is caused by the HP Virus, the Human Papillomavirus. And so it can be eradicated. It can be treated if lesions are discovered early. It is very easy to treat them. But if it is full blown cervical cancer, it is nearly always deadly."

The former First Lady made the statements during our discussion at the meeting of African Presidents' spouses at the Kennedy Center. She also said, "One of the advantages, really, of PEPFAR was that many countries, because the counties that got PEPFAR money had to design their own strategy. They had to design the strategy that they wanted to get health care out to their villages and out into the more remote areas. And so there are a number of clinics that are PEPFAR sites around Africa now that weren't there numbers of years ago. So we can add just the testing and treatment to an already established health care. But you are right, the treatment, if you do have cancer, you would have to go into the largest cities and even then they wouldn't have the kind of equipment that we expect to have in nearly every city in the United States to treat cancer. The great news is there are a lot of new, smaller technologies that are more affordable."

"GE, for instance, has a new small handheld mammogram machine that, if we can get these out around the world, we really will be able to spread the word and to make sure more and more women can be treated if they do find a cancer. But that is part of the problem, and one of the reasons that we chose cervical cancer as one of the cancers to try to talk about. Because when, if you are discovered to have early lesions, they are very easy to eradicate. And it is also very inexpensive to test for cervical cancer. You can just use vinegar to swab the cervix and you will be able to see the lesions and they will show up with that."

"So that's one of the reasons we are there. Part of the great news of this summit today is that over $200 million has been committed by different American companies and NGOs [nongovernmental organizations] on a lot of different projects, but some of them are health-related to try to make sure each African country can try to build the kind of health infrastructure that they need. Some of the other commitments have to do with agriculture. In many countries in Africa farmers are usually women. It's usually a woman's job. And so that meets two needs. It meets both the need to use women in the economy to have women have a role in the economic life in their country by farming, but also to feed people."

For me, the larger question is, why was the news of Bush's efforts in Africa either not as broadly known, or did the Bush Communications Department choose not to spread the news as it may have been a no-win situation?

Mrs. Bush refutes the later, saying, "I think they talked about it. I think they talked about it a lot. As you know, we went often. I went five times to Africa when George was President. He went two or three times, maybe. As you know, April, when you think back on it we had so many things—this is really the advantage I had of the First Lady. I could focus on just a few things. Look, every problem of the world comes to the desk of the American President. George had every problem on his desk. Of course after the September 11 terrorist attack you know there were just so many national security issues that he dealt with every day and that he thought about every day and that he worried about every day. So I can see why PEPFAR and different programs in Africa got lost a little bit in the coverage. Although many people, and people who are interested in global health or knew about global health, certainly knew about it." With the focus on Africa building from President to President, Mrs. Bush says, "I do think this country is heeding the call."

Syndicated talk show host and outspoken political critic Tavis Smiley says, "George Bush did not do a whole lot for African Americans across the board. No Child Left Behind, I think it was a joke. The one area where he does deserve credit is on his Africa policy. George Bush stepped up, certainly, to where other Republicans had not been. In some ways George Bush did better than some Democrats on Africa. He stepped up. He traveled to Africa. George Bush gets high marks, I think from a lot of people, on his AIDS in Africa policy. So he did a lot of good in that regard for brothers and sisters on the continent." But overall, Smiley weighs his efforts in the Black community, saying, "Bush did ban racial profiling. He did something. He didn't do enough or near enough. I don't think with Bush the good outweighs the bad. But he did do some good. Dr. King used to say all the time, 'There is some good in the worst of us, and some evil in the best of us.' Presidents are not incapable of doing good things even if their last name is Reagan or Bush."

Anyone privileged to live or work in the White House understands it is about wielding power to help people. That should be the overriding thoughts of most White House staffers and Presidents. But sometimes help can come in the form of acknowledgment of generations of oppression. February 27, 2004, was the day I was picked to take a leisurely stroll from the South Grounds of the White House with First Lady Laura Bush to the Corcoran Art Gallery across the street. There were sun-filled skies over Washington and temperatures that invited outside activity. The welcoming weather on that winter day gave Laura Bush an occasion to tell the Secret Service and the White House limo driver not to bother because we would walk the three city blocks to the Corcoran.

Despite her request, I watched as uniformed and plainclothes officers quickly dotted the path to the building just beyond the back of the White House campus. The walk began from the Diplomatic Entrance of the White House around the South Grounds out of the gates closest to the Oval Office. During the walk, Mrs. Bush invited me to tour the Quilts of Gee's Bend exhibit as a thank you for a reporter's luncheon that my company, AURN, and I hosted in her honor several months prior at Zola's (once located in the Spy Museum in Washington, D.C.).

Gee's Bend was named after Joseph Gee, the first White man to stake a claim in that remote area of Southwest Alabama in the early 1800s. The Gee family sold the plantation to Mark Pettway in 1845. Most of the hundreds of people who live in Gee's Bend today are descendants of slaves on the former Pettway plantation. Katie Mae Pettway resides in nearby Alberta, Alabama. At fifty-three she considers herself one of the youngest quilters of the area. She uses scraps from homemade dresses, old frocks, and some new fabric to create her master-pieces, which she "loves doing."

"It means a whole lot to me . . . it gives me peace, a good mind like if I am stressed or something like that, have something on my mind or worry I go to sewing it just gives me a lot of release. Matter of fact I love the sewing," says Katie of her passion. Pettway was at the gallery event in 2004. Nonetheless, she is a Gee's Bend–area quilt maker, estimating she has created about fifty-three quilts in her lifetime. She says it takes her four days if her mind is on it to several months if she takes her time to "quilt quilts."

Giving and receiving recognition is not a partisan action. Katie Mae Pettway is a Democrat who anticipated the First Lady's visit. "I am not a Republican. I would never be a Republican." But she was thrilled to meet the First Lady at the gallery event. "I never thought I would be able to see her . . . It made me feel real, real good. It did. It did." The ladies were more than satisfied with Mrs. Bush's appearance, but they were expecting more during the tour of the exhibit and the luncheon in the lobby of the entrance. Pettway said, "I was thinking I was going to see her husband, but I didn't see him. It was good to see her although I didn't see him. . . . We all thought we were going to see him." None of her quilts were on exhibit, but she was part of the group celebrated that day for her art. Pettway is also a descendant of the Gee and Pettway plantation by marriage. She says her late husband, Willie Dale Pettway, would tell her all the time, "We were bought people."

Mrs. Bush seemed to enjoy the exhibit as it was originally pegged as a birthday lunch for one of her staffers. It ultimately turned into a Black History Month event fraught with tears. On the walk to the Corcoran, Mrs. Bush and I talked about our grandmothers and their gifts of quilting. With two different life paths, we still had shared experiences. She told me her southern grandmother's quilts were very warm and even hot in the winter months as they were made from wool suits. I told her how my North Carolina grandmother would sometimes use the space of an entire room when making a quilt, spreading it out in its entirety. My mother recalled from her childhood that she would come home and could not get in the doorway because my grandmother would be framing her quilts.

We shared the stories of quilts made out of love that were used for practical purposes during the cold winter months in the South. Then the conversation set the stage for what we were about to view. The Gee's Bend quilts were made with love, telling a story of perseverance during slavery to the civil rights era. Each quilt was unique in its presentation, and some were primitive. Yet the quilter's heart and imagination compensated for less than perfect borders and the crude, hand-sewn stitching. These exhibited, priceless pieces were a welcomed and dramatic contrast to the sewing machine and Euro-American quilts that sell for thousands.

Now this functional art that once covered a bed and warmed bodies was on display in the nation's capital. That quilted fabric on exhibit was originally made to survive the cold winter months, but they were dusted off and meticulously hung in five rooms of the Corcoran. One quilt made of red, white, and blue patchwork enlisted the words *vote* throughout the piece. Another quilt told of a widow's tale. An Alabama woman wanted to remember her late husband at night so she quilted his soiled denim work clothes. The cloth included the dirt he toiled in while gathering sweet potatoes from the fields. Corcoran exhibitors said the widow could still smell the sweat from his labor and hints of the sweet potato fields when she slept at night. It was her comfort in knowing her husband was still there.

The exhibits showed strength and survival through the hands of African American women with generally untold pasts. Walking through this exhibit, taking it all in, gave us an understanding of the process of how an artist feels while making a priceless work. Each quilt signified the pain-filled stories of African American southern culture. In most cases that culture bore a past filled with hatred and oppression of a people who wanted nothing more than to rise from tyranny.

As the First Lady and I walked the rooms of the exhibit, I remember fighting back tears seeing these elderly women who were just so happy to get some recognition from the scraps of their hard-fought life. Every time we viewed a quilt, the women exhibiting their projects were joyfully and emotionally swept away with the First Lady's presence.

At the very end of the exhibit, five older women who previously displayed their crafts and were descents of slaves from Alabama's Gee and Pettway Plantations, enveloped Mrs. Bush in a huddle and shouted "Thank You, Jesus!" The moans from their cries reverberated throughout the rooms and brought so many to tears. It seemed the cumulative weight of their lives, at least for that moment, had been lifted by a bit of recognition.

These women, descendants of slaves, proudly displayed the bits and pieces intricately put together by hand, in most cases. Each piece was a witness to an American history often carefully tucked away in trunks and closets and only told during the winters when their warmth was needed.

I was moved, because for me the women, their struggles, their quilt making, and their ancestry as descendants of slaves caused me to tear up throughout the entire exhibit that ended with a major cry. I, too, am this part of America. I lay under that same fabric that they created so many years ago for their quilts. I am the descendant of a slave, five generations removed from Joseph Dollar sold on the auction block in Fayetteville, North Carolina, to the Brown family.

Months later, at the end of vacation season particularly for the President and his staff, race played the largest role it would ever play in the Bush Administration. It was a time when the recognition and help came ever so slowly in the time of pictures and instant media coverage. Kanye West even went on national television saying "George Bush doesn't care about Black people." During the end of summer, the storm of storms had hit and the Bush Administration was laid bare and exposed as hundreds of people were dying after the levy break in New Orleans.

That single comment spurred a discussion across the country about race in America and the hurricane victims. Bush later commented that of everything that occurred during his presidency, "It was a disgusting moment, pure and simple. I didn't appreciate it then [and] I don't appreciate it now."

Housing and Urban Development (HUD) Secretary Alphonso Jackson was responsible for trying to find housing for the displaced in New Orleans at the

rina. His department came up with a clearinghouse system to help
sing, but the system was not available until close to the end of the
Bush Administration. The Black HUD Secretary and former Texas neighbor
of President Bush strongly warned that people should be careful with their
words when calling his friend and boss a racist. "It is very important when we
start talking about the President not caring about Black America! That disturbs
me tremendously. And it disturbs me because I went to Louisiana, Mississippi,
and Alabama with him. And I saw when we hit the ground in Mississippi and
Louisiana his eyes bubbling up. I mean, he is compassionate."

According to Jackson, "I saw he was very angry with the way we responded.
And he said it was never going to happen again and he came back and we sat
at a meeting. He said, 'We didn't do what we should have done.'" Jackson remembers some people at the table said "no" and President Bush did what he
said he would do. President Bush put Fran Townsend in charge of finding lessons learned after the devastation, what was right and wrong. Jackson contends,
"If you look at the percentage, more White people lost their home than Black
Americans." He affirms what he believes: "It is not about race." Jackson said
sternly, but with a calm voice, "If we would have responded ten minutes earlier,
it would not have changed the general perspective."

Understanding the mind-set of the administration from the beginning, and
now looking at lessons learned, if the administration would have done the work
in the Black community and engaged the group more before the flood, the feeling might not have been as damning. It would have certainly been bad, but not
to the degree it was.

Condoleezza Rice said, "I dealt with Katrina, for instance, I spent a good deal
of time trying to help the administration recover from the images of poor Black
people being ill served. In fact, I was the one who put him in touch with the
NAACP. So I wasn't the Black Secretary of State or the Black National Security
Advisor, but I felt that when I had these special issues I could be involved in
those because I had a special perch for them."

That slow delivery of assistance to New Orleans by the federal government
surrounded a Republican ideology of states' rights, giving Louisiana the unwilling lead in the next steps of the aftermath. The Bush Administration was
working to fix the perception issue—a press relations nightmare—and simulta-
neously working to literally save and rebuild lives. The Treasury Department,
in the early days after the storm, was in a quandary of trying to locate folks to
help with the financial payments issue. Many residents who moved did not have
any identification, or even an address, as homes were either partially flooded or
totally destroyed. Tony Fratto said, "If your house has been wiped out and you

don't have a bank account and you rely on your Social Security payment, how do you get it? Where do you go? Where does that payment go? How do you pick up your payment check?"

There were so many people who connected with the victims left in the Ninth Ward. One of those people has a generational connection with the city that was underwater for weeks. Actor, humanitarian, and New Orleans native Wendell Pierce talked about the love he has for his community. "I was born and raised in Pontchartrain Park, which was a neighborhood that grew out of the civil rights movement of the 1950s. There was only one day out of the week that we could go to a park as African Americans in New Orleans, and that was on Wednesdays. The mayor decided to set aside two hundred acres where an African American subdivision—separate but equal—could be developed in post–World War II New Orleans. That neighborhood was called Pontchartrain Park, which is anchored by a golf course. Joseph Bartholomew designed it, and he designed most of the courses in New Orleans, but couldn't play on any of them because he was African American. So this was the first place that Blacks could purchase homes in post–World War II suburbia in the 1950s. My father had just come back from World War II and purchased a home there with the GI bill. What's so important about Pontchartrain Park is, although it grew out of something ugly—segregation—the pioneers of the neighborhood created a wonderful Black Mayberry that turned into an incubator of talent. The first Black mayor came out of Pontchartrain, "Dutch" Morial; his son, Marc Morial, also Mayor and National Urban League President; Eddie Jordan, the first Black DA; Lisa Jackson, former EPA Administrator; Terrance Blanchard, Grammy-award-winning jazz trumpeter, composer. Dare I put myself in there, in that number, the first family of Black journalism, the Dejoie family [pronounced Day-shwah] that owns the *Louisiana Weekly* lived in the neighborhood. At one point, per capita, it was the highest concentration of higher education degrees in New Orleans—97 percent of African Americans, 92 percent of home ownership, less than 10 percent poverty when in the city it was 28 percent poverty."

About ninety thousand square miles was under the federal declaration of disaster after Hurricane Katrina devastated parts of Louisiana, Alabama, and Mississippi. The George W. Bush White House was responding to two different situations. There was wind damage in Mississippi and flooding in New Orleans. In New Orleans the priority was to save lives and fix levees. For the smaller communities impacted by Katrina, it would be weeks and before they saw tangible help from Uncle Sam.

During that time, President Bush met with Federal Reserve B Alan Greenspan to find out what economic impact Katrina's de try. One problem already realized: a temporary disruption of ...luct. With that, the Department of Energy approved a six-million-barrel loan of crude oil from the Strategic Petroleum Reserve for ExxonMobil Corporation. The gas company had to repay the loan barrel for barrel with interest. It was so bad President Bush issued a mandate: "Don't buy gas if you don't need it." In the midst of the aftermath, the federal government took over 100 percent of the costs of recovery, relief, and security for the Katrina-affected areas for sixty days. The White House even took other nations up on offers to help in responding to Katrina's devastation. But Cuba's help was not wanted in the midst of the pain there. The White House rebuffed all of Cuba's offers for medical assistance and supplies. As a nation, it was painful for everyone, regardless of race, to see the images of such despair in such a prosperous country. It appeared as though those looking for help for days were mostly Black people.

Weeks after the levy break, I traveled to Mississippi with First Lady Laura Bush and Education Secretary Margaret Spellings. I got the first interview with Mrs. Bush after Kanye West made his statement. She was appalled, and she said so on the plane as we were flying back after viewing the devastation. Sitting beside the First Lady for the interview, she said to me on the way back to Washington, D.C., "I think all of those remarks were disgusting, to be perfectly frank. Because of course President Bush cares about everyone in our country and I know that. I mean I am the person who lives with him. I know what he is like. I know what he thinks and I know how he cares about people. I do think, and we all saw this, was that poor people were more vulnerable. They lived in poor neighborhoods. Their neighborhoods were more likely to flood as we saw in New Orleans."

But during that trip, the First Lady met with so many survivors who were being cared for and housed in several facilities, to include a church in Mississippi. One of those people was a Black mother who was so grateful for a mattress to lay her family on and a mom who had just given birth and was living out of a church after the disaster. Secretary Spellings, a close friend of the Bush's, wiped tears away while seeing those who were just grateful to be alive and were trying to put their lives back together, bit by bit. It was a tough road for The Big Easy. Even today the city is still working to fully recover.

On the first anniversary of the tragedy, I found myself traveling with President Bush and the First Lady on *Air Force One*. Fortunately, I was able to conduct a dual interview with the First Couple. President Bush gave me a tour of the family sleeping quarters before the interview and said to me that he wished there were more minorities in the Press Room. He added, "I am not pandering to you." I knew he wasn't, as we have had talks before on numerous occasions.

I was even his guest at his table for a State Dinner. But he was right. I have looked at that crowd in the Briefing Room, watching as reporters are getting seated, and more representation is definitely needed. The main reason: there are grassroots issues, minority issues out there that need to be highlighted. I'm there, and I of course do my best to raise issues, but I'm only one person. Logistically, I certainly can't even begin to cover all of the minority issues that plague this country.

It's unfortunate that this President's heart never came through during his two terms, largely because of the agenda and policies of those he worked with and those in his tight inner circle. Before my interview with him I did say that if the circumstances had been different, I could have been one of Katrina's victims. Like countless numbers of folks, I tend to wait out storms, expecting things to get back to normal once the sun comes out. However, this time that did not happen.

We landed in New Orleans, and as part of the presidential motorcade we drove the route of Katrina destruction, through the Ninth Ward, where we saw a sobering number of houses still tagged with spray paint that signified they either had no inhabitants or bodies needed to be retrieved. We also drove past the Convention Center and Superdome. I was in shock. I tried to remember I was there to report, but as a Black person it was difficult to separate my job from my compassion for these people. I was watching people who looked like me suffering unimaginable circumstances. It was much different seeing such devastation up close.

When the 2008 Presidential Election was underway, I was at the White House reporting from my small booth in the basement of the West Wing. There were other reporters there, such as Wendell Goler of Fox News, down the hall working to report on developments as they occurred. The air was heavy with expectation of something about to happen. That something we did not know, but there seemed to be so much hope for a day we had never seen before. Even the President and the First Lady and some senior staff were up late waiting for the election results. My worst fear was that it would be like 2000 all over again, no results that night. I just knew it would be drawn out. But it wasn't.

Normally the Bushes were in bed by around 9 p.m., but that night they were up and their residence radiated with light as everyone waited for results. Around 11:00 p.m., Wolf Blitzer of CNN announced the winner of the Oval Office. "Barack Obama will be the forty-fourth President." I could not believe it. I honestly did not think our great country was ready to make that choice. I just knew a White woman would be President of the United States before a Black man. I was in shock and immediately hurried out of my office down the hall to the Fox booth. I stood at the door and saw Wendell sitting there. He turned to me slowly, we hugged and started crying.

Within an hour of the announcement, a huge, spontaneous crowd had gathered in front of the White House. The folks who showed up looked to be mostly young White kids from area schools. Their excitement was palpable as some carried life-size cardboard figures of the new President, Barack Hussein Obama. Others were carrying red, white, and blue balloons. Despite the bitter cold, some of them even had their shirts off, apparently warm in their exuberance and enthusiasm for change. At several points in the evening, the crowd began chanting, "Na Na Na Na, Hey Hey Hey, Bush good bye." I noticed that the lights were still on upstairs, meaning that they had surely heard what was transpiring below. The crowd was growing and growing and the Secret Service watched carefully, only intervening once when a young man jumped the fence.

The next morning it was clear the American people had spoken the way all politicians recognize, with their votes. Now it was time for the sitting U.S. President to recognize and acknowledge the shift that Americans had demanded. From my vantage point of the Rose Garden, looking into the French doors of the Oval Office while waiting for the President to speak, I saw a very upset man. He was gesturing wildly, arms flailing as he passed in front of the door, visibly angry. All of a sudden, he turned and saw me standing outside, looking straight into the Oval Office at him. I had been caught watching, and I stood frozen. All of a sudden he lifted his arms and proceeded to "raise the roof." We both laughed heartily.

His gesture had totally changed the atmosphere, and his National Security Advisor, Steve Hadley, peeked out the door to see who had changed his mood. He saw me and smiled. Not long after that light-hearted moment, President Bush came out of the Oval Office and stood at the steps of the Rose Garden, in front of the podium decorated with the Presidential Seal. He made his statements marking the transition of Barack Hussein Obama as the forty-fourth President of the United States, the first Black President in this nation's history.

Political commentator Armstrong Williams contends, "Prejudice is a handicap. If we fail to see other's inherit worth and value as human beings—if we fail to treat others with the respect they ultimately deserve, we not only harm others but also ourselves and handicap our prejudice . . . We fast-forward to where we are now . . . to President Obama in my opinion personally sums up the potential for American Blacks and modern society as Justice Thomas. And to all the Justice Thomas haters, they need to remember, there is no Black Supreme Court—just the Supreme Court, that is responsible for upholding the Constitution and Thomas is part of that monthly calling. So American Blacks in the middle class is larger than any time in U.S. history . . . many Blacks have overwhelmingly benefitted by finding meaningful jobs and defining careers for them and their children."

Dr. Jeff Gardere said, "I think a lot of people see George W. Bush as being a caricature, but in fact, this is a very, very complex individual who I think perhaps had some issues with all the power, and the privilege he was given. Maybe [he] never wanted to be President, but felt that was the path he had to follow, that was his destiny. So when you tell me this idea that this thing of stopping and raising that roof, I think that was an acknowledgement to you and I think to the world. Here's a person who understands the significance of this first Black President . . . I think that the connection between George W. Bush and President Obama is that George W. Bush, fairly or unfairly, was seen as the butt of a lot of jokes and was disrespected in many, many ways by the public. President Obama has been disrespected in many, many ways because of his color, so I think that's where the connection is."

However, some of President Bush's welcoming of President-elect Obama may be his belief in a higher power and the practice of a favorite Bible verse, Luke 6:31: "Do unto others as you would have them do unto you." Tony Fratto said, "His [President George W. Bush] faith was very important to him," as he took his "best lessons from faith."

So in the interim in the transition to the forty-fourth President of the United States, President Bush marked history and was public in his welcoming of the new First Family. Since their exit from Washington, D.C., the Bush couple has resided quietly in Dallas, living a relatively quiet life. But they are getting back to work according to Mrs. Bush. "We are continuing to work on the four policy areas that were important to us when he was President. And one of them is global health because of PEPFAR, the President's Emergency Plan for AIDS Relief, that he started—that we launched in 2003 in Africa and has saved now millions of lives. I think the number today was nine million people in Africa are now on ARVs (antiretroviral) and living full, productive lives."

With the ease of a smile and a twinkle in her light blue eyes, Mrs. Bush confidently stated about their life after politics, "We are going to continue to visit Africa. We will continue to speak out about AIDS and Malaria and make sure PEPFAR and all the American aid to Africa continues because it is really important, and we want to continue education."

Meanwhile, back at the White House, Chief Usher, Rear Admiral Stephen Rochon, was given the task of making sure the next President's needs were met as he was coming to live and work at the White House, even including trying out prospective barbers. The Chief Usher position was created back in 1866 with President Andrew Jackson. Admiral Rochon said, "The most memorable time was preparing for the new President, the first African American President, in the White House. It was challenging. Unlike the Bushes, he was bringing in a young family, two darling little girls, and they had requirements."

Those requirements included making the house allergy-free for one of the children. (The Bushes had two dogs and a cat, so the residence had to be thoroughly cleaned.) Rochon says because this President likes to play basketball, a regulation basketball court was installed to replace the tennis court. Rochon was also charged with getting the "perfect" swing set for the girls. I recommended a Rainbow swing set since my girls have had one for years. We call it the "Cadillac" of swings sets, and that's the kind the Obamas ended up with.

It was clear that changes were being made across the country as well as in the most famous residence in the United States. A new era had been ushered in, and on Inauguration Day in 2009, after a mere two hours of ceremony, the transition was made.

A Black man was now arguably the most powerful person in the world.

7

PRESIDENT OBAMA

When he was a Senator, Barack Obama came with the Congressional Black Caucus (CBC) to the White House for a meeting with President Bush. It was one of those big meetings where the Congressional Black Caucus wanted to present their issues to the President, front and center. It was also one of the first meetings in Washington with the new "it" guy. Already the town was abuzz about this relative unknown running for President; after all, he had only just become a U.S. Senator. He hadn't even settled into his congressional office yet. Senior officials from Chicago came to D.C., contributing to the murmurs that politicos in town were unable to truly grasp. The challenge for these newbies was that they were trying to navigate their way around a town steeped in tradition and protocol. They were hesitant to become fully vested in the area because of the negativity they initially received, long before Obama had even announced his intention to run for President.

When the group of Black federal lawmakers came out of the West Wing to the bank of microphones known as the "Stake Out," I could not find the new guy in the crowd and was so exasperated that I called out to find out where he was. I mistakenly transposed his name. I don't know what I called him, but apparently he heard me. "Get my name right first," I heard from the back. Not surprisingly, he did not grant me an interview, but I found out later that President Bush did welcome him to Washington separately from the group.

To my surprise, I found that a group of lawmakers were not always as friendly toward Obama as one would have surmised. There was disd___ for the upstart freshman in Washington. The distaste for Obama was from ; include some members of the Congressional Black Caucus. The fir

successful run for then-four-term incumbent Congressman Bobby
in 2000. In a twist of irony, Obama lost the race, but he became a
political star in 2004, delivering the keynote address at the Democratic National
Convention, only the fifth African American to do so at that time. But the stars
lined up in 2005 for Obama to win the U.S. Senate seat left vacant by Republican Jack Ryan, who left after sordid details were released during his divorce.
Some very prominent veteran members of the CBC were not impressed with
Obama. He was a member of the esteemed group of Black federal lawmakers,
but he had a tough time.

According to a CBC member, Obama would never have time to present his
items at CBC meetings because he was on a different schedule than the rest of
the group, who were on the House schedule. They were unwilling to make
adjustments for him to speak on issues from the Senate side. Although there
were a few members who were his friends and remained loyal, the division in
the group was obvious, especially when it came time for his presidential run.
A large portion of the group supported his opponent, Senator Hillary Clinton.
That support was in part because Senator Barack Obama was not a known en-
tity. There was also skepticism about whether the country was ready for a Black
person to be President. That could be a problem for this rising Democrat who
was shaking up the Black establishment on the Hill. Obama strategically remembered who was friend or foe and remained mysterious to so many, including
the press, and he would only grant interviews to Chicago-related media, which
only helped build on the mystery surrounding him. Naturally, as journalists, we
wanted more, and the frenzy over Barack Hussein Obama ensued.

In October 2006, the Congressional Black Caucus Legislative Week was
under way, culminating in an elaborate dinner. It is a huge event in D.C., one of
the must-attend events, especially for Blacks. I got a call from Tommy Vietor,
the Press Secretary for Senator Barack Obama. I was actually shocked since
I'd been calling the Obama office constantly asking for interviews, only to be
turned away. Well, I was finally handed the golden ticket. Vietor invited me to
the dinner as a guest of Senator Obama. He had only one ticket, and that was
fine by me. I immediately said yes. This was a big deal, and euphoria kicked in
right away. Then I started to wonder why he would ask me to sit as a guest and
not any of his aides or a Hill reporter. I surmised my seating was meant to keep
chatter going about the White House prospects, and maybe they hoped for an
insight into some of the press chatter. Let's face it, I was the only Black reporter
working on urban news and very visible at the White House. That dubious
distinction worked for me and against me. This time, I wasn't sure which it
was. But that night while I sat next to Mrs. Obama, Senator Obama was mostly

working the room. When he finally sat down, someone was alway honestly felt sorry for him because I had seen before how the der office will eventually wear on the individual. There's no way around it. I did get a brief moment with him after I used the old trick of walking over and standing beside him. I knew that was the only way, and I certainly wasn't going to waste this invitation without some type of interaction. Understanding the dynamic of this country and how things had worked before, I asked him, "Would you consider being Vice President?" He politely chuckled, saying, "Why be Vice President when I can be President?" He did it with a smile and moved on, shaking the hands of others waiting nearby for a quick photo. But looking back and knowing what I know now, maybe the question was an insult. I was just trying to cover all the angles.

As folks whispered about the rumors and speculation of his future political plans, I knew that meant he was Oval Office bound, or hoped to be. I did talk to Mrs. Obama, and she admitted they had not discussed it yet as a family. That night Obama was the rock star, and you could see some members of the CBC were not happy with how much attention he was getting and the traffic jam around him. It turned out to be his night, not theirs as a group. That night it was obvious the crowd wanted him, and Obama fed on their attention. He was in his glory. And perhaps because of that, the division between Obama and some of the CBC grew wider. During the first term of the Obama Administration, then–Press Secretary Robert Gibbs was asked about the strained relationship with the CBC, and he said, "Now they have to call him Mr. President!"

On January 16, 2007, the challenge to reality as we knew it had come, the real possibility of the first Black U.S. President. It was the day a man perceived a novice took the national spotlight, just halfway through his first U.S. Senate term. Barack Obama announced his run for President in Springfield, Illinois, the home of one of the nation's most transformative Presidents, Abraham Lincoln.

That same day, civil rights leader Al Sharpton remarked at a Tavis Smiley gathering of Black leaders, televised on C-SPAN, "Just because he is our color does not mean he is our kind." The crowd roared with enthusiasm after the words left Sharpton's lips. Those were powerful words to ponder for me. "Our kind" translated into someone sympathetic and able to work for change on the plight of Blacks in America. As the Bible says, "The least of these."

Reverend Al Sharpton is now the preeminent civil rights leader for the Obama Administration. However, they did not know one another before the first presidential election. A relationship began to form before then-candidate Obama won Iowa. Since then, the two have bonded. Sharpton supports this

President for his historic nature, but he also lets him know when he feels there are problems or issues that need to be addressed.

So now, within the community, two men have been singled out for the distinction of "Black President." The first person, who eagerly accepted, was Bill Clinton. Clinton is a southern White Democrat who acknowledged his proximity to poverty growing up and brought African Americans to the table countless times. He has been credited with recognizing and validating the Black community after years of shameful White House neglect. Clinton was given the title at a time when the thought of a Black man as President was only a distant dream. So now, the first Black President is the leader of the free world. The Black community placed them both on a pedestal as one of their own.

Clinton continues to receive strong approval ratings in the Black community, with slightly lower numbers than his time as President. A 2008 National Opinion Poll conducted by the Joint Center for Political and Economic Studies found Bill Clinton's numbers for the first time were beaten only by Barack Obama. In 2008 Bill Clinton's numbers stood at 85.5 percent, slightly off from his high as President at 91 percent in 2000. Those 2008 numbers came after the subtle and overt racial conflicts during the Democratic fight leading up to the presidential primaries in 2008.

The Iowa win for Obama practically guaranteed smooth sailing toward the Oval Office. Governor Doug Wilder contends it set the pace for southern states to move in his direction. "In Iowa was the eye opener for South Carolina. Iowa caused South Carolina because when people there said 'you mean to tell me that a majority state of Whites and a majority voting population of Whites has chosen this man to represent them and us as the nominee of the Democratic Party, then we here in South Carolina, we can sell him to do the same thing.' That likewise affected what was happening here in Virginia. It made North Carolina change, and rather than for it be said that Obama lost and disappointed in New Hampshire. I think that to the extent he came as close as he did was miraculous, because any number of things were in play at that time. So I think up to that point he had not involved himself with race. The unfortunate thing was when Bill Clinton made a few of the remarks that he made, it reminded people of what was taking place, and a lot of people then took the positions that we're not going to allow that to play a role in our selective process."

When it comes to Presidents, candidates today and their relationship to Black America, Bill Clinton is still the measuring stick, which is a blessing and a curse. Clinton said, "Even though the main divisions today are not necessarily racial, although African Americans have overwhelmingly supported Democrats since the civil rights movement, and overwhelmingly supported President Obama, that this fight even within the Republican Party between the Tea Party and the other guys. . . . A lot of it is whether you favor the politics of *illogical righteousness or politics of inclusion*."

The nation was hypersensitive about race in the lead-up to the nomination. Mud was slung and fouls were called on the Clinton camp, the Biden camp, and almost every other candidate. Just after Obama captured the Democratic nomination in July 2008, the toll of how race played out in the campaign reared its head. What had held this nation together before, after some of the biggest upheavals, was now breaking apart. There were comments of "us versus them." There was upset over the preached word of a Black minister who intertwined a social message with God's word. There was upset over things like "let's take back our country." The levels of intimidation grew as folks were even carrying guns to Republican Party rallies.

Stevie Wonder, who had been around presidential politics for decades, candidly said in an exclusive radio interview I conducted that it is a "sickness." The "sickness" was the racial prejudice we were seeing from some who thought themselves well-meaning. Stevie went on to say, "If you have hate in your spirit, that is not of God. It just isn't. And I say that because a lot of people who say these things and say they are spiritual and religious and all that, it is just not true. You can't be. Sometimes you know I wish the world were blind because I think that we all have to be color free and see with our hearts. But that is just a wish that I have."

It was November 3, 2008, and the final campaigning was under way when tragedy struck. Barack Obama lost one of the major forces in his life to cancer. Tears were streaming down his face as he officially announced to a North Carolina crowd that he had lost his grandmother, a woman who helped raise him. Madelyn Dunham died that morning with Barack's sister, Maya Soetoro-Ng, by her side. That tragedy brought a closer inspection to Obama's diverse family tree. Obama, in efforts to make his comments heard on race, often used his White grandmother as an example of his ability to understand the issues of different races. Some critics were not happy about that analogy, but the President said, "The point I was making was not that my grandmother harbors any racial animosity, but that she is a typical White person. If she sees somebody on the street that she doesn't know (pause) there's a reaction in her that doesn't go away and it comes out in the wrong way."

I specifically asked the President, for this book, to "please share something you have not discussed publicly, a moment or moments you were discriminated against because of your color."

Barack Obama: "Well, I wrote a whole book, April, about growing up and how race affected me. And, I think, like every African American out there, there have been moments in my life in which I sensed that I was being judged by the color of my skin rather than the content of my character. But the truth is that I've always considered my race a source of pride and strength. I come from a mixed family of all different races, and I think that's made me appreciate more what it's like to overcome stereotypes and to knock down barriers or prove people's expectations wrong. But it has also taught me empathy and that deep down, we're all the same. We've got similar hopes and dreams. Obviously we've got different cultures and different circumstances, but our basic desire to have meaning in our lives, to raise our kids, to be in communities where we're making a contribution, to be respected and to have a sense of dignity and purpose in our lives, to work hard, to watch our kids grow up, to overcome hardships and sufferings—those things are what we all have in common."

So on November 4, 2008, Barack Obama became the first elected Black President. With the beginnings to fulfill past promises of the forefathers for all to be created equal, the rally of the Black community was slow to happen for Obama. But once the Chicago Senator captured Iowa in the caucus race, Blacks had taken note. House Majority Whip James Clyburn took a neutral stand but supported Obama for the Oval Office. Clyburn remembers that in March 2008 all hell broke loose for Obama. Two politically corrosive and potentially deadly issues became entangled; the breaking point had arrived. The sworn enemies of any politician—religion and politics—were handed to Obama at breakneck speed. The Jeremiah Wright controversy could have killed all political aspirations for Barack Obama, but he managed.

Congressman Clyburn grew up as a preacher's kid. He says, "I grew up in a parsonage. My father was a minister; I know what it is to go through that sort of thing. To know how religion—how important it is to the African American community. How controversial it is in politics. . . . It was his response to Jeremiah Wright and how he weathered that endeared me to Barack Obama . . . his survival of that made me a disciple!"

Dr. Martin Luther King Jr. said a man's character is proven in the midst of adversity. Congressman Clyburn said of the Obama race speech in Philadelphia, "I think that was the turning point of his campaign. He got some flak for that. One of the best speeches anybody could give . . . it will go down as one of the best political speeches of all time. Yet because of a little story told about his own grandmother, he got criticized severely. Everybody knows damn well what he was saying was true! He was sharing an experience. . . . That is what he was talking about, is our refusal to have an honest discussion on race."

Ultimately, America has the first Black President. But no matter who is President, the Black concerns should be at the forefront as well as Latino, Asian, Native American, and the list goes on. There will never be enough done for any one community by any single President.

Five days before the President-Elect's swearing-in ceremony, then Republican Secretary of State, Condoleezza Rice, remarked on the 2008 presidential contest, lauding "race really was not a factor." However, exit polls tell a different story. The Joint Center for Political and Economic Studies confirms that Blacks voting in the 2008 Presidential Election hit record highs of 13 percent or 16.6 million compared to 11 percent or 13.42 million in 2004. Those numbers shattered the previous record, post–Voting Rights Act in 1968. The obvious reason for the notable turnout: a Black man with a presidential pedigree had a real chance at leading this country.

From her antique-laden and highly secured perch at the State Department, Ms. Rice, the first African American female to hold the post, never divulged her choice at the polls months earlier. Rice did, however, say, "It is a remarkable journey that America has been on. I have always said America had a birth defect at its founding—great and high ideals about all men being created equal, and then slavery; and of course Civil War, and Jim Crow and the great civil rights movement. It's been a long journey. I think America is becoming what it claims to be, that we are overcoming our old differences."

The Obama Administration touts it lifted seven million out of thirty-two million from poverty throughout the Recovery Act in 2010. There are other accomplishments, like the killing of Osama bin Laden, health care reform, and putting the focus on civil rights through the Justice Department. They also tackled major issues like voting rights, gun control, immigration reform, raising the minimum wage, and equal pay for women, but race always found a way to dominate the landscape when it came to President Obama. It was a rising tide that lifted all boats, an agenda without specific targets for Blacks who were disproportionately affected by disparities in education, unemployment, health coverage, incarcerations, and the list goes on.

Secretary of State Colin Powell, July 20, 2010, said, "The election of President Obama shows what is possible in this country and has demonstrated that a Black man can achieve the highest position in the land. He was elected by all Americans. At the same time, it exposed the reality that prejudice and racism still exists in the country. So, we still have a long way to go, but increasingly, success along the way will be measured by performance, not racial identity. President Obama demonstrated that fact. We have to stop harping about race differences, without overlooking injustices. Let us educate our Black and Hispanic kids so they will have to be measured by their ability and performance. Politics are not frozen by the color of your skin. The opposition will go after you because they are the opposition. Welcome to politics!"

Reverend Jesse Jackson, however, a keen observer of the Obama politics, says, "No President has faced the level of hostile attacks personally than has President Barack Obama." Jackson defends that strong statement, saying they "question his birth, where he was born. Questioning his religion, which is always personal." It does not end there for Jackson; they "call a health bill a death bill."

But the politics for Barack Obama were new and never seen before on all sides of the spectrum to include the presidential inner circle of Black civil rights leaders like the late Dorothy Height of the National Council of Negro Women (who had interacted with Presidents since Roosevelt), Reverend Al Sharpton of the National Action Network, Marc Morial of the National Urban League, Ben Jealous of the NAACP, and Melanie Campbell of the National Council on Black Civic Participation. Some of the leaders saw the changing of the guard and knew they were on their way to be the Jesse Jackson of the Clinton years. Reverend Jesse Jackson, who had been on the Democratic and Republican presidential scene from LBJ to Clinton, was not a part of the Obama group to help discuss the plight of Black America. Former President George W. Bush did not enlist the help of Jackson, and neither did President Obama.

Jackson lost any ground he might have had when he was caught by a hot microphone talking about cutting the President's genitals off for discussing what was needed for young Black men. But former President Clinton did say of Jackson, "I think Jesse Jackson, whatever anybody wants to say about him . . . was the one African American leader that never, not a day in his life, would give up on poor White people. He went to Appalachia with me, remember, that night when we had that New Markets tour. He always thought Americans who are relatively dispossessed and working as hard as they can . . . should and could make common cost and I remember when he won in 1988, when he ran for President, it was 1984 or 1988 . . . I think it was his 1988 race. Whichever one, in one of those races, he won South Carolina, and got 59 percent of the vote . . . and it was an amazing coalition between African American voters and low-income White voters who believed—He grew up there . . . South Carolina . . . and they'd actually believed him when he said that he tried to get them a better deal. That's what America needs today . . . we need people talking to each other across these lines . . . and we need to do it whether we get votes or not."

White House staffers strategically understand the dynamics at play never to bring attention to the elephant in the room with Obama. TV show host Roland Martin says, "I think there's a clear reluctance on the part of this White House to overtly identify as African American." Martin firmly believes "issues of race are greatly downplayed." Race is an overwhelming part of his presidency even without it being said. It's undeniable that in some circles, Barack Obama is hated and vilified because of his race, even though he is technically a mixed race man. Racial hate is bred out of pure selfishness and ignorance. Another example is the disdain that followed Dr. Martin Luther King Jr. Reverend Jesse Jackson remembers the time and what was happening to Dr. King. "He was hated. He died a very hated man. He rose the next morning, as a man that we loved." Jackson equates it to the love we feel for a "risen Jesus."

The highly anticipated Election Day finally arrived. I remember driving in the Baltimore area, going to the polls early in the morning and standing for two hours to vote. Yes, I'm a journalist, but I am also a tax-paying American who works to be objective professionally, but privately that is another matter. I could interview a KKK member today and report the story objectively. With that said, I always (and always will) exercise my privilege to vote. My vote is personal, as all votes should be. What is unfortunate is that Blacks were typecast after that day. We are always thought of as Obama supporters just because of our race. But regardless of one's affiliation, the 2008 election was a major shift for our nation. Black districts saw swells of people going to the polls, standing in line for hours. I remember taking my elderly father to a voting precinct not far from my home. He also stood in line for more than two hours. The same scene was playing out around the country. I used the time wisely and talked with other folks who were in line and recorded their jubilation over what they thought would be a never-before-seen victory. Of course, they were right.

In battleground states like Florida, Ohio, North Carolina and Virginia, two-hour lines were the norm while states like Utah saw almost no lines. A democratic pollster said Arkansas and West Virginia have seen an influx of White voting, making those two states turn "redder" because of Obama. The reason is that race and politics are "the most dominant veritable in history, particularly in the South."

On Election Day, once Dad finished voting I moved on to the White House where I would stay for the rest of the evening to report on whatever the voters decided. Honestly, I thought we would see a repeat of the 2000 Florida debacle. Night fell, and I was camping out with other reporters in the White House as we waited along with the sitting President and the First Lady glued to their TV and surrounded by staffers.

I eagerly watched the election returns in my cramped booth, and finally at 11:00 p.m. the result was clear. If you weren't in Obama's hometown of Hyde Park in Chicago, the White House was the place to watch history. You could feel the new momentum and the excitement about the newness of what was coming. You could touch, feel, and taste it. It was real, and it was undeniable. When Wolf Blitzer made the announcement on CNN, I briskly walked down the hall to the Fox booth where Wendell Goller was working. I stood at the door and peered in. He turned in his chair and hugged me around the waist and began to sob. It was real for Wendell, but we never discussed that moment again.

The inauguration was next, and the presidency of Barack Hussein Obama quickly followed. It was amazing to be able to experience this change from the White House on election night. Even today the story is still gripping. Seeing it for myself, I remember being in the pool in the motorcade with President Obama the day before inauguration. We were off the record, meaning we were stopping at lights. We had finished covering the President's service event in a D.C. neighborhood. In my community we call it "the hood." The motorcade made us wind around the streets of D.C. right in the midst of the crowd. The President's car had a D.C. license plate with the number 44 on it. I remember the full motorcade was stopped in front of Union Station, and the crowds were converging on the Capitol just blocks away and the President was in his car and folks did not know it was him. But he could see the swells of mostly Black people there for him. I kept saying, "I can't believe they do not know it is him in that car." You could reach out and touch the exhilaration in the air.

This middle-class Black family moved into the White House, and America began to learn more about them. The Obamas came across as a young, hip family that just happened to live at the most famous address in the country. They seemed very approachable and accessible. Hip-hop sensation Derrick Watkins, better known as Fonzworth Bentley, was touring the West Wing of the White House when he spotted the First Lady and her new dog, Bo. It was such a casual, everyday slice of life except that here was the First Lady walking into the West Wing with pedal pusher denim shorts, a striped yellow and white shirt, and a side ponytail, walking her dog through the West Wing. Change had come.

Bentley says, "Here's the thing. What President Obama did for the hip-hop generation, he really represented someone whom they felt could speak and understand a little bit more of their language. I think that they felt that, here was someone really yearning and reaching out to them, and wanted to hear their ideas and wanted to get them involved in the political process."

In the weeks following, just blocks away from the Hyde Park in Chicago home of then President-Elect Barack Obama, Nation of Islam Minister Louis Farrakhan allowed the tears to flow during a taped conversation about the incoming President, a man he says he does not know. Fraught with emotion, Farrakhan held strong to the words, "That this great man has lifted all of us. The least little brother in the street was touched by him! They had a picture of him visiting a school, just maybe ten days ago. And, when you look in the eyes of the little children; how they look at him; and now, they are not thinking maybe I will be an athlete or an entertainer. But, because of him the sky is the limit for these children. That is a genie you cannot put back in the box anymore! He has impacted us in a way that no one in our history has impacted us. However, no matter what he does he can't be the burden bearer for us as a people. That's the job of our preachers, our activists, our leaders. He's given us hope. Now let's go out and lift our people up from where they are and not let them think because they have a Black man in the White House everything is hunky dory and now we won't have to work hard to help ourselves. We have to see this as an opportunity to advance the whole people by the work of all of us who work in the Black community. We have to lift our people up so that if this young man creates five million jobs, which ones of us will be able to take advantage of such an opportunity if we are dropping out of school or if the education is substandard? So, I am grateful to God for this young man."

The election was more than just electing a Black President, according to Minister Farrakhan. "I see more than a man becoming a President." I interjected with a simple, tear-evoking question at the Hyde Park Palace, "Is it God?" The minister responded saying, "I see the hand of God working with this young man."

Yet, Black America in some ways may look at President Obama as a sort of savior. Minister Farrakhan: "My hope is the Black community does not hope too much." But Black America has a shot at a potentially better life than before, according to Farrakhan. "Black people who have always been marginalized in this society can begin to think in terms of taking ownership of the country where we live."

During the first term, the administration took what many called an "umbrella approach." President Obama, exclusively for this book, answered a question on this very subject. He said, "I do think that a lot of the things that we've done that have had an enormous impact on African Americans sometimes haven't been framed as race issues because they're not. They're issues that all of us should be concerned about. So when we expanded Pell Grants to make college more affordable, African American and Latino kids disproportionately benefit from that because they're poor and oftentimes come from families where the parents didn't go to college. But that may not always be noticed because we don't frame it, per se, as an issue exclusively affecting one group."

"One thing that I think people haven't paid attention to is the degree to which we have reinvigorated the enforcement of our civil rights laws. You've got an Attorney General, Eric Holder, who has really strengthened the Civil Rights Division that has made sure that we take seriously the laws against discrimination. And we're going to continue to do so as long as I'm President."

"So there are certain issues like antidiscrimination laws in housing and on the job that obviously are directly related to race, and I think that a lot of my most important jobs and, frankly, one of the jobs of every President who is in here should be to make sure that everybody is getting a fair shot in this society."

But the historic examples of racial imbalances in this country are more prevalent today as the plight of Black America is under a magnifying glass because of who is leading the country, and what actions or inactions will be taken are also being analyzed because a Black man with an exotic name is the President of America. Examples of the imbalance on economics between Blacks and Whites were further highlighted by Thomas Shapiro of Brandeis University. At the National Press Club event he remarked that when Blacks suffer a job loss, they can sustain financially for three months, but Whites can sustain financially for four years, on average.

The Obama years have seen a roller coaster of unemployment numbers when it came to the Black numbers that outpaced the overall rate by almost double. The numbers grew during the George W. Bush years but exploded after Obama assumed the helm, during the Great Recession. It's unfortunate but true that "when White America has a cold, Black America is on life support." The Labor Department numbers are astounding. Black teen unemployment numbers in October 2009 rose to 41.3 percent, while the overall unemployment rate was 10.2 percent. That same month saw Black overall numbers at 15.7 percent, the Hispanic overall numbers were 13.1 percent, and the overall teen number, 27.6 percent. In March 2010 the Black unemployment rate was 16.5 percent compared to the overall rate of 9.7 percent. The Obama Administration was working hard to lift the country out of the inherited recession with mixed results. Jobless numbers during the Obama years were more than double that of the Bush years. The Labor Secretary commissioned a study, *The African American Labor Force in Recovery.* The findings are things we already knew. The study reveals Black workers are more likely to be employed in the public sector than are either their White or Hispanic counterparts. In 2011, nearly 20 percent of employed Blacks worked for state, local, or federal government compared to 14.2 percent of Whites and 10.4 percent of Hispanics. Blacks are less likely than Hispanics and nearly as likely as Whites to work in the private sector, not including the self-employed. Few Blacks are self-employed—only 3.8 percent reported being self-employed in 2011—making them almost half as likely to be self-employed as Whites (7.2 percent).

In 2012 the administration's efforts began to gain ground—a million jobs were created. Labor Secretary Hilda Solis acknowledged during an interview with me for American Urban Radio Networks that half of that number went to the Latino workforce. A large number of those jobs created were skills based. It is unfortunate that these numbers remind me of something awful that then Mexican President Vicente Fox, during the Bush years, said: Mexican immigrants to the United States "take jobs that not even Blacks want to do."

Then 2012 was the height of the presidential reelection campaigning and minorities were worried about their plight, but not enough to move toward Republican candidate Mitt Romney, who made very little effort to appeal to Black America. On the other side of the aisle, President Obama gave an interview to Oprah Winfrey and also participated in over thirty-five interviews with Black media since his official early April reelection bid.

The Obama Administration has been strategic in ways to help the Black community and its workforce in the long run, understanding any targeting will cause immediate backlash from the extreme right. Examples are the Recovery Act and efforts to build infrastructure, which also benefitted Hispanic workers. Issues of health and wellness are other efforts to bolster the wellness of seven million uninsured Blacks to get them healthy and on their way to being "workforce ready." The Affordable Care Act had a reach far beyond just the obvious of paying for insurance. Health care was the focus of the President's fourth nighttime press conference. For the first half-hour he droned on for an average of seven minutes per reporter on the health care and insurance reform. The ultimate goal was that 97 percent of the American public would be covered by some sort of insurance. But it was a "big fucking deal," as Vice President Biden inadvertently acknowledged to the world. The bigger issue for the President: if he got this through when other Presidents could not, he would have unmatched political capital, but Republicans would make sure he would never be able to redeem it.

In the summer of 2009 health care was overshadowed when the President took his last question from his hometown paper of the *Chicago Sun Times*. Lynn Sweet asked a question on race after seeing the story on Harvard professor Skip Gates's arrest. At least three others, including myself, had some form of the question. The President has typically been able to dance around race questions, but for whatever reason he spoke directly on the matter, taking ownership of what happened.

LYNN SWEET: *Thank you, Mr. President. Recently, Professor Henry Louis Gates Jr. was arrested at his home in Cambridge. What does that incident say to you? And what does it say about race relations in America?*

PRESIDENT OBAMA: *Well, I—I should say at the outset that Skip Gates is a friend, so I may be a little biased here. I don't know all the facts. What's been reported, though, is that the guy forgot his keys, jimmied his way to get into the house; there was a report called into the police station that there might be a burglary taking place. So far, so good, right? I mean, if I was trying to jigger into—well, I guess this is my house now, so— (laughter) it probably wouldn't hap-*

pen. (Chuckling) *But let's say my old house in Chicago—* (laughter) *here I'd get shot.* (Laughter) *But so far, so good. They're, they're, they're reporting. The police are doing what they should. There's a call. They go investigate. What happens?*

My understanding is, at that point, Professor Gates is already in his house. The police officer comes in. I'm sure there's some exchange of words. But my understanding is, is that Professor Gates then shows his ID to show that this is his house, and at that point he gets arrested for disorderly conduct, charges which are later dropped.

Now, I've—I don't know, not having been there and not seeing all the facts, what role race played in that. But I think it's fair to say, number one, any of us would be pretty angry; number two, that the Cambridge police acted stupidly in arresting somebody when there was already proof that they were in their own home. And number three, what I think we know separate and apart from this incident is that there is a long history in this country of African Americans and Latinos being stopped by law enforcing disproportionately. That's just a fact.

As you know, Lynn, when I was in the state legislature in Illinois, we worked on a racial profiling bill because there was indisputable evidence that blacks and Hispanics were being stopped disproportionately. And that is a sign, an example of how, you know, race remains a factor in the society. That doesn't lessen the incredible progress that has been made. I am standing here as testimony to the progress that's been made. And yet the fact of the matter is, is that, you know, this still haunts us.

And even when there are honest misunderstandings, the fact that Blacks and Hispanics are picked up more frequently, and often times for no cause, casts suspicion even when there is good cause. And that's why I think the more that we're working with local law enforcement to improve policing techniques so that we're eliminating potential bias, the safer everybody's going to be.

All right? Thank you, everybody.

Now, did he need to go that far in his statement and description of what he thought happened? President Obama knew the subject of the inquiry, racial profiling, and the person thought to have been profiled enough to elaborate on the subject that was usually taboo. To the surprise of the press that evening, the President stepped out on his own beyond the protection of his inner circle, who obsessed over never "amplifying" race.

In July 2009, a selection of beer was strategically placed on the patio table outside the Oval Office to indicate a tone and conversation as a casual civil dialogue. President Obama was brokering what was a racial peace deal of sorts. On occasion, President Obama publically embraces what is irrefutable—he is a Black man in America and that comes with some of the commonality of the other brothers and sisters across the country.

However, the topic shifted on November 25, 2009, at the India State Dinner. Tareq and Michaele Salahi, D.C. area socialites, crashed the White House party with little effort. It became a media sensation, and the image of the couple being announced as they entered was repeated on every network and news outlet. It revealed an embarrassing breach in security. As the State Dinner for the Prime Minister of India spotlighted the issues of security, the unspoken concern for this President's safety is always something on the minds of Obama Administration staff and others.

The White House Chief Usher, Rear Admiral Stephen Rochon, says he works to "try to forget" the chaos but "remembers like it was yesterday." He says it was an "interesting" evening. Rochon says, "I did not know who they were. I met them by accident actually before the State Dinner occurred. And normally I would see everyone coming through the doors to be seated for dinner and be able to check them off a list. As much as I begged for the list, I was not provided one by the Social Secretary. But it shouldn't have even had to have been an issue at my level. They got past, which is unusual, the Secret Service long before it was even me checking a list at the actual entrance into the dining hall which was set up in a huge tent on the South Grounds."

Michaele Salahi even interrupted Admiral Rochon as he was talking with Robin Roberts of ABC News. He ultimately saw the Salahis trying to leave the tent where the State Dinner was soon to be served. The admiral said, "You are leaving so soon." He remembers Mrs. Salahi's exit strategy was to say she received a call indicating her mother was ill and she had to leave. She said they knew the way out and would to exit. Admiral Rochon could not let them exit alone and had to escort them to their vehicle.

It was a huge news story, and the questions started inside and outside the White House. Admiral Rochon remembers being called into the Social Secretary's office and asked if he knew the couple. He said no. But the questions came fast and furious in the Briefing Room, too. I began a line of questions over two days in which Robert Gibbs, the White House Press Secretary, tried to shoot me down. I was getting too close to the truth, and he was fiercely defending his colleague, going as far as blaming the Secret Service. In the past it had been successful to marry both the White House Social Office and Secret Service at the gate. The line of questioning was unavoidable.

Q: I wanted to ask about another subject, the State Dinner last week with India. The White House has asked the Secret Service to investigate the incident, what went wrong. As part of that review, will they just be reviewing what the Secret Service did or will they also take a look at White House staff, Social Secretary's Office, and see whether they made mistakes, as well?

MR. GIBBS: *I will check with folks here. My understanding is that the Secret Service will look at what the Secret Service did.*

Q: *But do you think the White House staff should be looked at, as well? There were guests who came to this event who say that at previous dinners there was somebody from the Social Secretary's Office there who was checking names. That's not really the responsibility of the Secret Service.*

MR. GIBBS: *No, but, Ed, understand that the individuals that are listed weren't on any list. I think the Secret Service, through the director, has admitted that somebody who wasn't on a list and wasn't waved in was allowed into an event that clearly he said shouldn't be, and that no call or reach-out ever came to anybody in terms of staff from the Secret Service about whether or not there was confusion on a name on a list.*

Q: *At previous dinners, there was somebody from the White House staff there checking names. So if they had been there and these people were not on the list, they might have caught them.*

MR. GIBBS: *But, again, Ed, I assume in absence of somebody being there—because they're working telephones in the White House—somebody would have checked. Again, I think the focus of the investigation at this point is on the fact that none—that name wasn't on a list, that name wasn't waved in, but that couple got into the White House and I think that's what the Secret Service is rightly focused on in their security investigation.*

Q: *Follow up. Normally in the past, before this administration came, there was always a checks and balances type of system at that gate with the Social Office, as well as the Secret Service—*

MR. GIBBS: *I think that's what Ed just asked.*

Q: *That's what I'm saying. And you're saying—*

MR. GIBBS: *This is a follow-up or—go ahead, I'm sorry, I didn't mean to interrupt.*

Q: *Again, there's always been a series of checks and balances. And if there was a concern from the Secret Service, they would always relay it back to—it was a back and forth between the Social Office and the Secret Service.*

MR. GIBBS: *What I'm saying . . . what I said to Ed was . . .*

Q: *But let me finish, please—*

MR. GIBBS: *No, no, no, but let me—I think the question was asked, so let me reiterate my answer. Again, April, none of that relay happened, right? None of that relay happened between the Secret Service and the Social Office, whether or not the Social Office was standing at the gate or whether or not somebody was sitting in their office at the White House.*

Q: *If you would allow me to finish, you can understand what I'm saying. The relay did not happen because that person was omitted at the gate from the Social Office. The way we understand, that person—*

MR. GIBBS: Omitted?

Q: That person was fired earlier in the year. So—

MR. GIBBS: But again, April, you can ask it seven ways. The answer continues to be, the relay didn't happen because somebody was or wasn't there. The relay didn't happen because nobody picked up the phone to relay the information. I mean, I appreciate the observation that somebody could or could not have been at a certain gate. But again, you could pick up the phone, just like I can pick up my phone in the office and relay you, April. You don't have to be standing in my office for me to convey information to you. I think the—

Q: So are you saying that the Social Office does not have any responsibility in this at all?

MR. GIBBS: April, there's an investigation that's ongoing into the actions of what happened, and I'm going to wait for that to be completed.

Q: The reason why we are questioning the Social Office and the Secret Service is because in the past, both have worked in conjunction and successfully were able to protect the President of the United States without anyone coming in. And now because the Social Office did not have that other layer of checks and balances there, this happened. And people are questioning why this White House is not putting the onus some on the Social Office, as well.

MR. GIBBS: I'm going to let the investigation put the onus on where the onus should be. But what I'm simply doing is explaining to you a series of facts that include the notion that if somebody was confused about whether or not somebody was on a list at a guard tower on the exterior perimeter of the White House, and there was a question, generally somebody could pick up the phone and ask. I'm saying that—I'm saying that the Secret Service, in the statement that they released a few days ago, acknowledged that that didn't happen and that that was a mistake.

Q: The whole process has been changed at that gate from now on. Will the Social Office be working in conjunction with the Secret Service now?

MR. GIBBS: I think first and foremost we're going to go through this investigation, and I would refer you to the Secret Service about operations that might change at that gate.

Q: And the last question. People were saying that the President was never in danger, and many people have said that is not true. They got in—

MR. GIBBS: Who's "many people"?

Q: People here, Secret Service. These people met with the President. They shook the president's hand. Who's to say they did not have some kind of—granted, they didn't—but hypothetically, what if a person had walked in and could have done something to the President? The President—do you—

MR. GIBBS: This hasn't happened before. (Laughter.) I appreciate the opportunity to indulge in a grand hypothetical.

Q: Has the President remarked on this at all?

MR. GIBBS: Look, I think the President shares the concern that the director has for how this happened and how we can remedy it from happening again.

Q: Is he concerned about his safety with this?

MR. GIBBS: No.

Q: Have you heard him say anything, is he angry or is he as incredulous as the average American is that people could just walk right into the White House like this?

MR. GIBBS: I think the President—look, the reason there's an investigation is the President and the White House has asked for that to happen. So I think suffice to say the President is rightly concerned about what happened last week.

Q: Have you actually heard him say anything about it?

MR. GIBBS: I have not heard it, but it's been relayed to me.

Q: Can you confirm whether or not charges will be filed against this couple?

MR. GIBBS: That is not a power bestowed on me as the Press Secretary. I know they've—according to media reports, they've been interviewed by the Secret Service. I think that's a decision that would be made by the Secret Service and the United States Attorney in that area.

During the exchange with Gibbs, Democratic strategist Donna Brazile would text message me on my Blackberry during that line of questioning and even the week prior, asking, "Why was [Robert] Gibbs so disrespectful to you?" It was obvious to me, but I worked to grin and bear it as I had to work with him to get to the principle, the President. I had been asking for an interview of the President for months, and I needed him. Little did I know that morning when this all blew up, he had submitted to the White House scheduler my request for a presidential interview. It was bad, really bad. But the worst was yet to come! Is there retaliation by the White House for some questions and manipulation in the spin of some stories? The answer is yes. The next round of questioning was what was captured on television and was a low point for both Gibbs and me. It was December 2, 2009, and here is the transcript.

MR. GIBBS: Yes, ma'am.

Q: Has there been any concerns about Desiree Rogers's performance prior to this instance?

MR. GIBBS: No.

Q: No one has questioned the President or told the President that she is a very last-minute person, poor planner?

MR. GIBBS: No, I think you—you all have been to and seen, either whether you're part of a pool, whether some of you have been to receptions, the remarkable work that they have done in pulling off a lot of events here. The First Family is quite pleased with her performance, and I've heard nothing uttered of what you talk about.

Q: Well, what about the issues of her being in fashion spreads early on in the administration? Did you put the brakes on that? I mean, that is—it's been raised, it's now public, you saw it in the magazines, her pictorials. You saw her on the cover—

MR. GIBBS: I get Sports Illustrated at my house. I don't—I don't get—

Q: But could you talk . . . seriously, could you talk about that? I mean, was there a concern in this White House that she came out being . . . some might have called her the belle of the ball, overshadowing the First Lady at the beginning—

MR. GIBBS: I don't know who "some" are. I've never heard that.

Q: Well, it's been bantered around Washington, and it's been in circles . . . Democratic circles as well as Republican circles, high-ranking people.

MR. GIBBS: April, that's not a station I live in in life—

Q: . . . administrations as well.

MR. GIBBS: No, I understand.

Q: Just answer the question, please.

MR. GIBBS: Are you done speaking so I can?

Q: Oh, yes, I'm done now, yes.

MR. GIBBS: Excellent. I've not heard any of that criticism. I've not read any of that criticism. The President, the First Lady, and the entire White House staff are grateful for the job that she does and think she has done a terrific and wonderful job pulling off a lot of big and important events here at the White House.

Q: Did she invite herself to the State Dinner or was she a guest—did the President invite her, or did she put her—no, that's a real—do not fan it off. I'm serious—no, seriously.

MR. GIBBS: Jonathan.

Q: No, no, no, did she invite herself, or did the President ask her—her name was on that list, and Social Secretaries are the ones who put the names on the list. Did she invite herself or did the President . . .

MR. GIBBS: Was she at the dinner? April, April, calm down. Just take a deep breath for one second. See? This happens with my son, he does the same thing.

Q: Oooh . . . Don't play with me, I'm being serious. Do not blow it off.

MR. GIBBS: And I'm giving you a serious answer. Was she at the dinner? Yes.

Q: Was she an invited guest?

MR. GIBBS: She's the Social Secretary. She had the primary—

Q: Social Secretaries are not guests of the dinner.

MR. GIBBS: She is the primary—for running the dinner. I'm going to get back to weightier topics like ninety-eight thousand men and women in Afghanistan. Jonathan, take us away.

Q: All right, April, please forgive me if I ask this question.

It was like salt in an invisible White House wound with each response. The questioning stemmed from sources and got too close, and Gibbs, the presidential mouthpiece at the time, struck back fiercely to protect his colleague. I remember being so angry after the briefing and remained in my then-fourth-row end seat and was asked to come to Gibbs's office by then-Deputy Press Secretary Bill Burton. At first I said no, but then I decided to go to his office. It was ugly. I was asked to apologize, saying I disrespected a hardworking Desiree Rogers and I disrespected the First Lady. That line of questioning was about protection of the First Family. I did apologize in efforts to calm the situation, but it was not about offending them. But I also said major Washington insiders are finding it disturbing how he disrespects me in that room. Gibbs said, "Tell them to talk to me. I will talk to them."

I never revealed to him who any of those people were. All of my questioning was about getting to the truth and why the ball was dropped. Anything could have happened. But not long after that briefing, the original clearance procedures for White House guests were reinstituted to include the Social Office and the Secret Service working together. Both Gibbs and I were bashed by the public. Each of us had a job to do, but at the end of the day we moved on and actually were better in the Briefing Room together.

The Comedy Central cable channel picked up the exchange, and it went viral. I soon found myself on the receiving end of negativity. I was warned by several Washington insiders and some folks in Chicago that an Internet campaign would be targeting me, and it did. It's difficult being on the receiving end of such hatred, but I'm in a visible position, and I can't avoid certain topics for fear of backlash. I have to do my job.

The next summer was horrific for the Obama Administration. One of the worst things that could happen did. A southern civil rights activist was fired by the Agriculture Department who conferred with the White House after receiving inaccurate information from then NAACP President Benjamin Jealous. The NAACP had denounced the statements of former Georgia Agriculture employee Shirley Sherrod at a March Freedom Fund Dinner. On tape, which was taken out of context, Sherrod said she withheld the "full force" of her position because a White farmer, asking for help, was acting superior. The full forty-three-minute tape showed her comments were part of a racial redemption story. Consequently, after reviewing the entire tape, the NAACP retracted its original statement, but it was too late. The damage had been done after pressure from right-wing columnist Andrew Breitbart, who thought he had something.

Jealous had been trusted by the White House and unfortunately did not perform his due diligence. The NAACP held an emergency meeting on their involvement in the recent national controversies on race. The civil rights organization called in retired Board Chair and Civil Rights Activist Julian Bond for a session of senior staff and the organization's executive board. Jealous was admonished for his lack of accuracy.

Shirley Sherrod knows of racism, as her father was killed during a dispute by a White farmer over livestock. She said her father worked his land for the betterment of his family, but at the same time he was beat down by racism. She says, "My father was murdered in 1965. He was farming and he defiantly faced discrimination. You know the house they're living in now, it's not the house they wanted to build. They wanted to build a house made of brick, but they were told by the county supervisor that a Black man could not borrow money to build a brick home . . . so they had to build a house made with block."

Later, being a sum of her experiences, Shirley Sherrod and her husband, Charles, fought on the side of the Black farmer for years, and in 2009 she became the first African American to serve as the Georgia State Director of Rural Development in the U.S. Department of Agriculture. Understanding racism was a huge dynamic in this situation that trickled down with negative results. Mrs. Sherrod spoke exclusively about her conversation with President Obama after her wrongful firing, saying, "As I tried to say to him on the call that we had, I really don't think that he nor the Secretary fully understand what we're dealing with here. I don't think either one of them has had the experiences that would allow them to fully grasp what we're dealing with here. So I guess it makes it a lot more difficult for them, to even look at how to deal with it."

During the conversation, the President worked to reinforce his understanding of the situation according to Mrs. Sherrod. She said, "You know the President kept telling me, if I read his book, and some of the things I was talking about, as I was doing those interviews that I would see that he would understand. He hasn't lived like some of us live, and he's probably, and I'm not saying he hasn't lived this way, in order to be able to understand, but hey, you've gotta get down to—I don't know—You just have to talk to some people other than the folk around you, to try to help him better understand it. And you know, in talking to the Secretary. He didn't—he also didn't have these experiences, and I think he didn't grow up around Black people. And not that you have to grow up around us to be able to fully understand, but they just . . . I don't think they've had the kind of experiences out here that some of us could help them to better understand, with more conversations, with a few little visits here or there . . . to understand, what this life is like."

Not only was the NAACP disappointed with Jealous, but so were officials within the White House who ultimately fired a public servant who should not have been let go. The federal government has tried on various occasions to compile a consulting package to draw Sherrod back to work with them, but so far she has not returned to the USDA.

An intense debate on race rose to the level of the White House in February of 2012. The news coverage was overwhelming from the re-creation of a 9-1-1 call where you hear someone scream out for help and then a gunshot. The rally cry from Blacks over what was perceived as blatant racial profiling went out. Trayvon Martin was killed. Many think it happened because he was a Black teenager wearing a hoodie and walking a path that was in an area that had been burglarized. President Obama addressed the incident, saying, "It was a tragedy." But what punctuated the President's statements was that Obama said, "If I had a son, he would look like Trayvon." The media played along with this coy dance. What did he mean? What do you think he meant?

But as the focus was on the semantics of what the President said, an intentional movement had begun. The hoodie crusade even made its way to the White House. A Chicago preacher wore a hooded sweatshirt to a prayer breakfast at the White House in an effort to keep the national spotlight on the shooting of Trayvon Martin in Florida. John R. Bryant, a Bishop with the African Methodist Episcopal Church in Chicago, said President Obama did not say anything about his attire, even as he shook his hand.

The weekend of the George Zimmerman verdict in July 2013, the NAACP Convention ironically was in Orlando, Florida. There was a pall over that convention. Folks around the nation felt justice had not been served. Black and White people and the colors in between were in a state of shock and disbelief after the Zimmerman acquittal that Saturday night. The irony was U.S. Attorney General Eric Holder was expected in Florida that Tuesday, days after the verdict. The NAACP found that Black males ages fifteen to nineteen were eight times as likely as White males of the same age and two-and-a-half times as likely as their Hispanic peers to be killed in gun-related homicides in 2009.

Reverend Al Sharpton, the NAACP, and others called for peace as the process played out, and people listened. Six days after the verdict, the President made a surprise visit to the White House Briefing Room. Reporters scrambled to get in the empty seats. After he spoke of the process, he elaborated on his previous statement by saying, "Trayvon Martin could have been me thirty-five years ago. The African American community is looking at this through a set of experiences and history that does not go away." So the President initiated a program to focus on preventing more of these incidents through My Brother's Keeper, a plan that pulls government agencies together to help cut into jail time and death for at-risk minorities, particularly Black males. It is a national security crisis issue since 25 percent of the Justice Department budget alone is allocated for jails and prisons. They are a lost group, not viable for employment or military, and potentially will end up dead or in jail.

The issue of reparations for Black farmers was a long, hard-fought one that finally came to fruition in December 2010. President Obama signed into law the payment by the federal government. Press Secretary Robert Gibbs at a White House Briefing said the movement on the funding is "much deserved" and "justice that is overdue" has come after almost two decades dating back to the Clinton Administration. President Obama signed into law a $1.15 billion measure to fund a settlement initially reached between the Agriculture Department and minority farmers more than a decade ago.

Shirley Sherrod gives the history of the Black farmer, saying, "When they started out, initially as sharecroppers, and then trying to do what every other American did, they tried to acquire land to make a better life for their families. And they worked against all odds. They did what I feel is an excellent job of working hard, and buying land." Sherrod says of the nation's Black farmers, "Well, when you look at all that Black farmers have done, since slavery, during slavery of course, where the land and so forth, and afterwards, actually trying to make a life, for themselves and their families, through farming, and then all of the discrimination that they experienced in doing that, I think that this country should really be up in arms, and feel bad about what happened, and what has happened, and therefore, should feel some sympathy, if you want to call it that, or some—but they should make some effort to try to right some of the wrong."

President Obama solidified his given moniker as the Civil Rights President when in 2012 he stood on the side of equality for the LGBT community. The President said during an interview, "I have stood on the side of broader equality for the LGBT community. I thought civil unions would be sufficient. That was something that would give people hospital rights and other elements that we take for granted." The LGBT community embraced the President's decision even though it did not change any laws. A magazine even proclaimed the forty-fourth President the "First Gay President," a label placed on him because of his support for the rights of that community. Meanwhile, the White House was quick to reply to the title by calling him the "Rights President."

BARACK OBAMA: "I continue to be optimistic about the future. The country is getting more diverse by the day. Young people I think have much more tolerant attitudes about racial differences than in the past. We're a polyglot society. Kids of every race listen to every kind of music. They interact in the workplace and in their communities in ways that they haven't before. And so I think that the trend lines are good."

"The key is going to be making sure that, first of all, we're expanding opportunities for all people, because I do think that racial tensions worsen when people feel like they're stuck and they're not getting a fair shot, and they're more likely, then, to turn on each other sometimes instead of working together to try to overcome the barriers to opportunity. And so I want to make sure that we're putting the economy in a strong place where I think this next generation that naturally wants to get beyond some of the racial divisions of the past is also feeling optimistic about their futures."

"And the other thing is we still have certain communities that are locked into cycles of poverty that have to be broken, and we've got to be willing to take those on systematically. I think we've learned some lessons from the past. We're not interested in programs that perpetuate dependency. We have to make sure that taxpayer money is well spent in providing opportunities, which is why the focus on education is so important."

"But we have to have a determined effort to tackle those communities that feel locked out and have been locked out for decades now, and generations in some cases. And that's not always easy to do because, frankly, our politics sometimes treats those communities as hopeless. But when you've worked in those communities like I have and you see all the talent that's there and the young people who are filled with potential and promise and really want to do the right thing, but just don't have good guidance and an easy path to success, it makes you that much more committed to making those investments."

"And I do think that for the African American community, sometimes I've gotten criticized by certain commentators for emphasizing individual responsibility and talking about the need for young African Americans not to use barriers of race or poverty as an excuse. I emphasize those things not to let the larger society off the hook for the legacy of slavery and Jim Crow and discrimination, but rather to give those young people a sense of agency, that they can do things for themselves, and that no matter how tough their circumstances, there are choices that they can make to stay in school and to apply themselves and to seek out adults in school or in church or in communities that can give them guidance, and to hold off on teen parenting and to avoid self-destructive behavior."

"There's no getting around the fact that these kids have greater challenges than a lot of other kids do, but that doesn't mean that they can't make better choices and can still make it. And that's something that I'm going to continue to use the bully pulpit to emphasize."

When it is all said and done, where is the President on his achievements and disappointments as the forty-fourth occupant of the White House? He commented on that when I interviewed him for this book.

BARACK OBAMA: I'm a firm believer that the most important thing that I can do for all Americans, regardless of race, is grow the economy. And when I came into office, the economy was in a freefall. The fact that we reversed that and have now created 7.8 million jobs over the last forty-four months has had a huge impact on everybody, but also obviously has helped the African American and Latino communities in significant ways. We also made sure during the depths of the recession that we kept seven million people out of poverty by expanding programs like food stamps, unemployment insurance, the earned-income tax credit, and a range of other measures.

Now, obviously, that means we still have a lot more to do. And one of the things that we've tried to accomplish is to take the limited resources that we have and make sure that we're doing a better job with programs that can help the hardest-hit communities. Programs like Promise Neighborhoods, where we pool the resources from all the agencies that are going in, provide technical assistance to make sure that we're creating the kind of holistic strategies that help kids learn in school, help them get to college, help attract new businesses, and help create jobs. And over the next three years, I intend to build on the successes we had and expand that to more cities.

APRIL RYAN: What's your greatest disappointment on race during your administration?

BARACK OBAMA: Well, this is really the flipside of the same coin. My biggest disappointment is that we have not grown the economy faster and created more opportunities for the American people to work their way into the middle class. Part of it is we had a big hole to dig out of and a lot of people are still struggling because of that.

But part of it, frankly, has been the stubborn resistance of Congress. We know, for example, that if we rebuilt our infrastructure—our roads, our bridges, our schools, our airports—all across the country, that we could be putting people back to work right now. A lot of those folks are people who were working in blue-collar jobs in construction and would provide opportunities for young people, particularly minorities who may not have planned to go to four-year universities, to still get good work experience and solid middle-class jobs. This didn't used to be a partisan issue, but the Republicans in Congress have been resistant to such measures.

We know that, because of sequestration, the economy has grown slower than it should have, and that means that there have been a lot of people who work for government contractors or federal employees have been really hard-pressed, and that's had an impact on African American and Latino communities.

We know that early childhood education would be the single biggest investment that we could make in promoting opportunity, particularly for poor children and poor minority kids. There are models out there that work, and what I've said is we need to expand those programs for every child in America so that they're prepared when they get to school. So far, at least, we haven't gotten traction from Congress on that issue, but the good news is that we have the tools to make these things happen. It's just a matter of getting beyond this attitude that somehow the market alone is going to take care of these problems—because historically, whenever we've seen great strides in the minority community, it's been because the economy was growing faster. But, it was because we were

*also making sure that people were equipped to take advantage of new opportunities in
new sectors.*

*And we've got to break the isolation of too many minorities who, whether they're living
in inner-city areas, on Indian reservations, or in barrios along the Southwest border,
we've got to break down the barriers that prevent them from accessing these new opportunities in this new economy.*

I asked Tom Joyner his thoughts about the importance and significance of the
Barack Obama Presidency. He replied, "Besides the obvious, him being the first
African American President of the United States, he has done a great job. He
turned around the auto industry, he had bin Laden killed, he passed Wall Street
reform . . . he passed the stimulus package, and he passed the health care reform
. . . But for some people it still isn't enough. They can't handle all that coming
from a Black man . . . and on top of that he's strong, he's vibrant, he's got swag-
ger. There isn't a Black man in America who can't relate to what happens when
you bring too much to the table when you're on the job. Someone will try to cut
you down, and the Big Chief is no exception."

Joyner has his finger on the pulse of Black culture and gives interesting insight into what he hears daily as he travels around the country and puts on his
popular radio program. So I wondered what he thought were areas that Presidents in general should address when it comes to Black America.

He said, "If I had my own bucket list as to what I wish the President could
do for Black people before he left office, I would ask him: One, to pay full
tuition for every Black child from a family who's a descendant of slavery,
entering their freshmen year at a college or university in 2016. I'd ask that he
pay for two full years at a mainstream institution with the balance being paid
by that college, and all four years if the student chooses to attend an HBCU.
Two, pay off the mortgage for every Black family with kids. These two actions
will dramatically reduce debt and give people a chance to breathe, get their
bearings, and begin on a more even playing field. This will be the answer to
reparations, and in my opinion, this doesn't even come close to paying the
true debt owed to Black people in this country. But it will say to every family
who is trying to do the right thing, we support you and we are giving this to
acknowledge that you were debilitated by the actions of this nation's government even beyond the signing of the Emancipation Proclamation and Civil
Rights."

Since I'm closing this book with a Presidential "Race" Report Card, I asked
Joyner how Clinton, Bush, and Obama fared when it came to addressing the
issues of Black Americans.

"I know the records will show how much both these Presidents did things for Black people, and they did. President Clinton and Hillary were certainly friends to African Americans. President Clinton made himself accessible to Black people, and because the economy was so much better during his administration, it was a good time for most Americans including African Americans. He also appointed nine Black cabinet members. Before he was elected Blacks had never held as many high-level cabinet positions. President George W. Bush had several Black appointments as well. But that doesn't mean he was empathetic to the needs of Black people in the country. It's like that person who swears he isn't a racist because he has a Black friend. It's about more than the people you associate with. It's about policies you put in place to empower Black people."

I thought a lot about his response, and those of the many others I consulted, as I pondered on the grades I would assign to the three powerful leaders that I have had the pleasure of covering closely on a daily basis.

THE PRESIDENTIAL
"RACE" REPORT CARDS

We have entered into a new era in this country, a time where minority births now outnumber White births. According to the U.S. Census Bureau, minorities made up 50.4 percent of the country's population under the age of one on July 1, 2011. Of course, that means the end result is that non-Hispanic Whites are projected to become a minority by 2050 (according to Pew Research Center projections). It shows that the times, and the population, are changing. It has taken decades to get to this point, but now it means there's a real shift in the makeup of our country. So there needs to be a shift in Washington to allow for a more diverse representation of the shifting demographics.

The first presidential term of Barack Obama was a very mixed bag because the initial euphoria was unimaginable. Here you have a Black man who made it to the highest office in the land, a feat most thought was a long shot, the impossible dream. Expectations were high, even extreme, because many viewed him as a savior. But as his tenure moved into a second term, it appeared that the issue of race was off the table. That has drawn ire and criticism from Black leaders including Ben Jealous of the NAACP, who wanted to march to get the Obama Administration to take note. The Congressional Black Caucus was clearly upset but had to manage their expectations. So unfortunately the progress was very slow when it came to targeting help for Blacks, particularly on the job front. There was even a Labor Department study on Black employment that told what we all knew. There are disproportionately high unemployment numbers in the Black community.

Bob Johnson conducted a study on racial attitudes, and he says, "Black people still feel that great sense of hope in Barack Obama. However, I think that you have to temper that with some of the harsh facts of economic life for Black people." The other side of the equation, Johnson points out, is that there is "double unemployment, a wealth gap, less growth in Black business opportunity, and less access to capital."

I've been working in this business for many years, and Washington is very much a White-male-dominated town that has yet to fully embrace racial change. The elitism, classism, sexism and, yes, in some instances racism is institutional and hard to change. But I am so glad there are folks like Steve Thomma of the McClatchy News Service, the President of the White House Correspondents' Association, who have the courage to take the stand to shed light on the darkness.

During the one-hundredth celebration of the White House Correspondents' Association dinner, he took the bold step of acknowledging that a Black man—Harry McAlpin—was shunned decades ago by this prestigious and elite group of reporters, who then were all White men. It took genuine courage to make that announcement. When he did that, every Black reporter who ever covered that beat was thankful and overwhelmed with emotion for the recognition of the terrible wrong done to McAlpin so many years ago. So what really has changed since then?

As I have seen presidential administrations come and go, I can assure you that each incoming Commander in Chief has the best of intentions. Each one has seemed very earnest and eager to do the best job he could. And while that's noble and admirable, when it comes to the issue of race in a country that was populated by immigrants, we should be doing much better than we are. As an educated, enlightened, ethnically diverse population in the twentieth century, we should be able to deal with the past and look toward the future, a future where everyone is treated with respect and dignity, regardless of color. Of course, that has to come from the top—the President of the United States.

Certainly we can, and will, make changes on a local, state, and sometimes even national level, but until it's addressed and properly handled by our federal government, change will continue to be slow. It's been five decades since King's famous speech occurred in the nation's capital, and still surveys show that minorities (specifically African Americans) continue to be treated differently than their White counterparts. So with the inevitable changes in our country's population makeup, racial inequity is an issue that should be addressed sooner rather than later.

As a Black woman who cherishes her bird's-eye view of our federal government, I remember that first day when I stared with awe at the White House and all it symbolizes. I was sure that once I walked through those doors, I'd see that things were changing, that there was hope for a government that wanted to represent all people. However, as I watched each President get sworn in and take office, it only took a few months before the good intentions gave way to political favors and party tradeoffs. Until we have a President who bravely tackles the race issue the way Harry McAlpin faced his challenges, our progress will be limited.

I talked earlier in the book about a Presidential Report Card. I have closely covered three Presidents and their administrations, on a daily basis, and I have conducted many interviews and posed countless challenging questions. So I'm grading each of them on how they handled the issues during their time in office. While each man had often very different issues to handle, I took a close look at how their policies and procedures positively or negatively impacted African Americans and other minorities in this great country.

PRESIDENTIAL "RACE" REPORT CARD

Bill Clinton
OVERALL: B+

A   Administration Diversity
B   Apology/Reparations (Black farmers payout)
A   Domestic Outreach
B   International Outreach
B   Jobs/Unemployment

George W. Bush
OVERALL: C–

A   Administration Diversity
C-   Apology/Reparations
F   Domestic Outreach (Katrina deaths)
A   International Outreach (HIV/AIDS in Africa)
D   Jobs/Unemployment (Recession)

Barack Obama
OVERALL: B+

A   Administration Diversity
A   Apology/Reparations (Black farmers payout)
A-   Domestic Outreach (At-Risk Youths, Civil Rights)
B   International Outreach (HIV/AIDS in Africa Ebola)
C   Jobs/Unemployment

EPILOGUE

After the historic results of the 2016 presidential election, April Ryan has found herself in the middle of a few controversies as she tries to continue doing her job as a White House reporter, despite the challenges of an adversarial administration. In this updated edition of The Presidency in Black and White, *she provides insight into those tumultuous few months and how it has impacted race relations in the United States. She also describes her observations of Obama's time in office and even gives an early look at Trump's impact on race in America.*

* * *

Since writing this historic book, so much has happened. I am now covering my 4th U.S. president with twenty years of White House experience under my belt, but things have changed. The divide is great and maybe even greater than before. I am speaking of the racial, religious, cultural, gender-related, and many other divides that have bubbled to the surface in the most hurtful of ways. That pain has forced us, all of us, to compare what has happened, what is happening, and where we are headed as a people. This is not conjecture or a myth. The racial dynamic in this country ebbs and flows. I liken the analogy to a rubber band. In better times we are able to stretch the rings of integration and racial harmony, but when the rubber band of history recoils, the chasm of racial hurt and negativity is more pronounced than ever. Particularly now as this nation, the United States of America, has a controversial new leader, the polar opposite of the previous president, the first Black United States President, Barack Hussein Obama.

Former President Obama's rise to the Oval Office created an openly demonstrated angst by some of the other races, particularly among some Whites, for his ascension to the highest office in the land, an office a Black person could previously only hope and dream of. I have always referred to this phenomenon as a "Blacklash!" This Blacklash has come full circle with the rise of a novice to political office, number 45, former businessman and now President Donald J. Trump. His name, his brand, has now extended to the White House. He appealed to people who felt left out and left behind over the past eight years. African Americans and those from other cultures heard what was believed as code while others heard something that made them feel like they were part of the equation again. The reality is that even though it is 2017, Black people and many other groups have seen this before. What is so painful for some this time is that over the previous eight years, many learned of historic racial struggles but never actually felt the sting of racism. Others were lulled into a false sense of societal growth and progression, and naturally assumed that the atmosphere of acceptance would have enough momentum to sustain long after the first Black president left office. That is far from what has happened.

* * *

Just two days before Christmas 2016 and well over a month and a half after the November 8, 2016, presidential election, I took time to pull my thoughts and jumbled emotions together, to openly discuss what had taken place in the highest office of our country.

Thinking back to the early hours of November 9, hours after all the polls had closed in the United States and its Territories, and the Electoral College numbers were favoring Donald J. Trump as the next President of the United States of America, the flood of feelings from countless voters who had been lulled into a predetermined outcome here in the United States and globally were caught off-guard by the unexpected results and the social media firestorm shifted into high gear. That sentiment even permeated the usually stoic and objective television and cable news anchors and pundits as they tried to make sense of it all. Not only was the public confounded, but so were those whose job it is to make sense of it all, to put it into perspective.

I had this feeling much earlier in the year, after Donald J. Trump had announced his candidacy. I kept telling friends and colleagues that he could very well be president. Most of them just pointed at the poll numbers and didn't take my prediction seriously.

Eight years prior, it had been almost the exact opposite. People were clear in who they supported, even exuberant in their zeal for the charismatic Black man with the nontraditional name, very different from the White founding fathers who came before him. In 2008 the nation was on the cusp of a drastic change of the system with new blood, something not seen before and outside of the thinking of the traditional Washington Beltway insiders. Barack Obama was not considered "the establishment," and historically that usually resonates with both parties.

Beyond the historical precedent his presidential win solidified as the first Black man to hold that office, there were many more changes to come and some were much more subtle as he ushered in an era that fulfilled America's longing for something new. After eight years of waning popularity for George W. Bush and his often rocky tenure, America was primed for a President who would make changes to the system. And of course, it was assumed those changes would last forever. However, in the lead up to the November 8, 2016, general elections, "hope and change" that won the previous election swung like a pendulum in the opposite direction. The direction was themed "Make America Great Again."

On November 8, even before the polls opened, in my mind, heart, and soul, I knew that what I had been feeling was not a fluke. It was stronger than ever. Hillary Clinton would not win. I was not a predictor of doom. In my profession I couldn't give my own opinion, but I understood intrinsically the issues on the table and I knew she wasn't hitting them the way people wanted. It was about the economy, but wasn't. It was about immigration reform, but it wasn't. It was about other issues, but it wasn't. What it boiled down to was the distinct divides in this nation and the widening of those lines. The "us versus them" mentality that we have seen in previous campaigns had become even stronger and could no longer be ignored. We had been here before and not many people wanted to venture down this road of conversation. Too many people shied away from the inevitable, but it was, and is, real. We taste it, smell it, breathe it and even bathe in this competitive matchup every four years.

Ultimately, Hillary Clinton won the popular vote by about three million, but the Electoral College, an archaic system created by the framers of the constitution in 1787, gave the Oval Office to Donald Trump. At the polls, people held their noses and cast their vote for the lesser of what they thought were two evils. Hillary Clinton wanted to show that taking the high road was the right way to go. In doing so, she allowed a bully to define her and her campaign without providing a much-needed response. She allowed him to repeat the phrase "Crooked Hillary" too many times, and soon she was smeared with more than just the dirt of her husband's past.

Former Secretary Clinton hoped to prove that she was much bigger than the gutter tactics of her opponent. Heck, he was (and still is) a ruthless businessman who thumbs his nose at the traditions of the game of politics. It was a game he was determined to win, and win he did. But Mrs. Clinton adhered to the Michelle Obama mantra before it inspired the nation, "When they go low, we go high." That's a noble sentiment, but when you are from an area where you have to fight continuously for everything in your life, you intrinsically know that you must address a bully head-on. That's something Hillary Clinton would not, or could not, do.

She received the support of Blacks, women, Latinos, and others, but the real fight was to gain the Obama Coalition. One stumbling block—we are still in a time where many people do not feel a woman should lead, much less be President of the United States. How passé. People did not want to re-elect the Clinton dynasty, thought to have its own set of rules, allegedly able to skirt around laws and policies. And, lastly, Hillary Clinton embraced the Obama Administration, one of the most successful presidencies of modern times. Yet, if she was elected the thought was it would be a continuation of his term, a Black man who many never wanted in the Oval Office in the first place.

No matter the history and her pedigree, she was tainted and whatever chink in the armor was there, Donald Trump would exacerbate, making her untouchable for those who chanted the slogan, "Make America Great Again." Even many of the "Never Trumpers" changed their tune in the blink of an eye toward the New York real estate mogul. The nation was stunned, with many in the fetal position for days and even weeks after the election, not understanding how the division and even subtle code words of hate could win over experience and reliability. Interestingly enough, just weeks into the presidency of Donald J. Trump, one of his kingmakers, a high-ranking Republican, told me just before the Conservative Political Action Conference (CPAC) that his conscience was bothering him. I said it was not time for buyer's remorse and advised him to fix it and pray.

That fix could be in the people who the President is surrounded by. As I sit in this unique perch as a White House correspondent with a clear view right in the center of the political machine that takes over (or remains) after every four-year cycle, I realize that longevity has its place. I've seen people come and go, and even some come back again. At first it seems odd, but then it makes sense that an administration would want to rely on institutional history and the knowledge that those who have worked in the White House before will have a good understanding of what it takes. That has been true for people like former National Security Advisor Susan Rice who formerly worked in the Clinton administration as well as former Secretary of State Hillary Clinton who was a First Lady and then became the Secretary of State for Barack Obama. Now there is even a reality show star who was once a Clinton White House staffer and was fired, and she came back to a much higher post in the Republican administration of Donald Trump. People come back one way or another.

Recently, I spent some time in the Manhattan home of singer and icon Harry Belafonte and he said, "Dr. DuBois, the great intellectual in the Black community, once said that true liberation will come for Black people only when things in America get more painful." He went on to say this pain perpetuates radical activism that effects change. Belafonte is a firm believer that "what Trump does, by his existence, is to no longer blur the lines."

On January 20, 2017, because of the drastic pivot in ideology, philosophy, and just about everything we had known for hundreds of years, I had to watch the last minutes of the historic presidency of Barack Hussein Obama. I saw the couple leave their home of eight years as I stood on the highest level of the constructed metal and wood staging that had been erected for the press. They did not see me, but I made it a point to get a prime vantage point to witness it all. I filmed it, every moment of this tall, proud man and beautiful, strong woman who had captured the world for a historic period of time. I watched two people who looked like me, close to my age, so similar yet so different.

Since the beginning of my reporting at the White House, it has always been about the transfer of power at the Capitol, but this time it was different. I watched the hopes and dreams of my ancestors, the unreal belief that after over 245 years of slavery, this would ever happen. I watched President Barack Obama and First Lady Michelle Obama leave the White House for the last time. As I hovered a few feet away just above the North Portico entrance by the windows of the State floor, I could make out figures still inside, standing in front of the window. It was Dr. Jill Biden and Vice President Joe Biden. It became even more real. I watched as history came to a close. What I saw was love overflowing between the President and the First Lady as they were leaving the White House for the next chapter in their young lives. But before that, an odd moment occurred, one that would foreshadow many more to come.

The couple came face to face with the man who had led the movement to rebuke his presidency and even his legitimacy as an American citizen. President Obama was genuine and gracious to the incoming First Couple, and the Trumps were too in return. It was a barebones staff at the White House and that became quite evident when Mrs. Obama struggled to figure out what to do with the big blue Tiffany gift box that had been presented to her by Melania Trump. She held it like a hot potato, passing it around in her hands and then behind her until President Obama took it inside and gave it to a staff member.

I watched the Obamas welcome in the new tenants of 1600 Pennsylvania Avenue, the Trumps. I had to see this. Why? Because of the history. Both men, opposites on the political spectrum and in rhetoric, were cordial to one another and moved forward to keep the democratic process intact, something our forefathers etched on paper long ago.

On that day, at 12:01 p.m., a new marker was set, the post-Obama era. What will it look like? The answer came almost immediately with issues of immigration, a travel ban, and many families living in terror that loved ones will be sent to home countries because of citizenship issues. Muslims are now concerned with not being able to get into this country and Blacks are struggling with what law and order looks like now. Jewish Americans are concerned with the rise of anti-Semitism. The nation is on edge.

With all this swirling around, I wanted to know about President Trump's "Black Agenda" as he talked of an inner-city fix on the campaign trail. After less than a month on the job, President Trump spoke and the world watched, listening carefully to his comments on fixing the inner cities. During an afternoon press conference, literally pulled together in 45 minutes, I asked a few questions in the East Room for the first Trump solo press conference on February 17, 2017.

TRUMP: Go ahead.

QUESTION: Mr. Trump?

TRUMP: Yes, oh, this is going to be a bad question, but that's OK.

QUESTION: It doesn't have to be a bad question.

TRUMP: Good, because I enjoy watching you on television. Go ahead.

QUESTION: Well, thank you so much. Mr. President, I need to find out from you, you said something as it relates to inner cities. That was one of your platforms during your campaign. Now you're --

TRUMP: Fix the inner cities.

QUESTION: -- president. Fixing the inner cities.

TRUMP: Yep.

QUESTION: What will be that fix and your urban agenda as well as your HBCU Executive Order that's coming out this afternoon? See, it wasn't bad, was it?

TRUMP: That was very professional and very good.

QUESTION: I'm very professional.

TRUMP: We'll be announcing the order in a little while and I'd rather let the order speak for itself. But it could be something that I think that will be very good for everybody concerned. But we'll talk to you about that after we do the announcement. As far as the inner cities, as you know, I was very strong on the inner cities during the campaign.

I think it's probably what got me a much higher percentage of the African American vote than a lot of people thought I was going to get. We did, you know, much higher than people thought I was going to get. And I was honored by that, including the Hispanic vote, which was also much higher.

And by the way, if I might add, including the women's vote, which was much higher than people thought I was going to get. So, we are going to be working very hard on the inner cities, having to do with education, having to do with crime. We're going to try and fix as quickly as possible— you know, it takes a long time.

It's taken more a hundred years and more for some of these places to evolve and they evolved, many of them, very badly. But we're going to be working very hard on health and healthcare, very, very hard on education, and we're going to be working in a stringent way, in a very good way, on crime.

You go to some of these inner-city places and it's so sad when you look at the crime. You have people—and I've seen this, and I've sort of witnessed it—in fact, in two cases I have witnessed it. They lock themselves into apartments, petrified to even leave, in the middle of the day.

They're living in hell. We can't let that happen. So, we're going to be very, very strong. That's a great question and—and it's a—it's a very difficult situation because it's been many, many years. It's been festering for many, many years. But we have places in this country that we have to fix.

We have to help African American people that, for the most part, are stuck there. Hispanic American people. We have Hispanic American people that are in the inner cities and they're living in hell. I mean, you look at the numbers in Chicago. There are two Chicagos, as you know.

There's one Chicago that's incredible, luxurious and all—and safe. There's another Chicago that's worse than almost any of the places in the Middle East that we talk, and that you talk about, every night on the newscasts. So, we're going to do a lot of work on the inner cities.

I have great people lined up to help with the inner cities. OK?

QUESTION: Well, when you say the inner cities, are you going—are you going to include the CBC, Mr. President, in your conversations with your—your urban agenda, your inner city agenda, as well as—

TRUMP: Am I going to include who?

QUESTION: Are you going to include the Congressional Black Caucus and the Congressional —

TRUMP: Well, I would. I tell you what, do you want to set up the meeting?

QUESTION: — Hispanic Caucus —

TRUMP: Do you want to set up the meeting?

QUESTION: No—- no — no. I'm not —I'm just a reporter!

TRUMP: Are they friends of yours?

QUESTION: I'm just a reporter.

TRUMP: Well, then (ph) set up the meeting.

QUESTION: I know some of them, but I'm sure they're watching right now.

TRUMP: Let's go set up a meeting. I would love to meet with the Black Caucus. I think it's great, the Congressional Black Caucus. I think it's great. I actually thought I had a meeting with Congressman Cummings and he was all excited. And then he said, well, I can't move, it might be bad for me politically. I can't have that meeting.

I was all set to have the meeting. You know, we called him and called him. And he was all set. I spoke to him on the phone, very nice guy.

QUESTION: I hear he wanted that meeting with you as well.

TRUMP: He wanted it, but we called, called, called and can't make a meeting with him. Every day I walk and say I would like to meet with him because I do want to solve the problem. But he probably was told by Schumer or somebody like that, some other lightweight. He was probably told - he was probably told "don't meet with Trump. It's bad politics."

And that's part of the problem in this country. OK, one more.

The first few months of the historic Trump administration were more than anyone expected. At issue, a man with a business approach, working to fix the ills of this nation. What is worse, he has a different take on how to "Make America Great Again." Neither he nor many of his top tier staff and cabinet have any experience in governance. So needless to say, it has been hit or miss a lot of the time on domestic and foreign issues. The tension in the White House and beyond is thick, so thick you can taste it. For some it is a bologna sandwich, for others the perfect Russian caviar they have been yearning for but never expected to taste.

When it comes to those of us embedded in the White House, the press, the White House Press Corps, the relationship has left a lot to be desired. There were terse words for our group of about 150 or so. Quickly, our ranks expanded to numbers that would make the fire marshal cringe as newcomers crowded into the already small press room. Yes, we have seen the crowds before at heightened news moments and over time the normal rhythms of the room would return. The Trump press office and even the President himself wanted to bolster the crowd of stalwart news agencies to other groups not known for reporting "actual news." Some could even call the newcomers "fake" and "very fake." It is not unheard of for administrations to favor news groups from their region or town, but this was different. Some of the attendees are from controversial blogs known for spewing hate, the kind that the history books recall from an ugly, tainted past.

We scratched our heads during those first days, weeks, and months, wondering if we would actually be kicked out of the briefing room to make way for these newcomers. I think that did not happen because the American public would have cried foul. Really, when you review the love/hate relationship people have with the press, the bottom line, the press is needed because people want to know what is going on from trusted, objective sources. And at the end of the day, it is not about us but about accurately informing the American people of the happenings in the highest office in the land.

We had several champions for our cause including Senator John McCain, a hero no matter his party affiliation, who took a stand not necessarily *for* us but *about* us. The stand was for supporting the First Amendment, the Freedom of the Press. We are built into the Constitution and the framework of the nation. The veteran senator knew if the press was "suppressed," that would be the classic definition of a "dictatorship." This former prisoner of war who had seen unspeakable atrocities when he was held captive understands what oppression and dictatorial behavior means and looks like.

He has expressed cautious concern in a very matter of fact way on the Sunday news shows and beyond. It took strength to do that because in some instances he would stand alone as many political colleagues inside of his party and outside of it would not support his claim. They were concerned that they could be ostracized and even worse, talked about, ridiculed, or even tweeted about by number 45 himself. People really are afraid of those tweets and the venom that follows from his constituents. He is the savior for many who want to "Make American Great Again." For me, I am just doing a job, covering a president as I have done for many years, asking questions on issues that in some cases expose right and wrong.

As all this was taking place, the administration was manic with the deluge of daily work. Just weeks after the Obamas left, it felt as if the West Wing was on steroids because of their approach to handling the business of America, particularly as to how the press was covering them. Then there were those legendary tweets that set the world on fire. President Trump and his strategically timed tweets are as dangerous as they are divisive and have created a culture on social media that pits people against one another due to race, religion, class, and political party. The timing for those missives is uncanny, early on weekends after watching the morning news shows or at other times after the airing of a TV program that strikes a nerve. In almost every category, the president's tweeting has created an "us versus them" mentality. This energy is unsustainable.

Since working in the media, I used to laugh at the jokes that we were "media slime," but this administration wasted no time sharing terse words about us, from Steve Bannon calling the press "the opposition party" to President Trump saying we are "the enemy of the people." These words from the administration have led to a disdain from some on the right who feel this president has all the answers. This feeling and the acting out has not been good for our nation. Taking it a step further, the claim of dossiers and keeping tabs on the press in the whisper campaigns against us were not right either. Every day it is like waiting for the next shoe to drop. We have no clue what will happen or even what to expect. Stressed and overwhelmed are just a couple of the feelings I've dealt with in this new atmosphere.

Some contend that the press is at war with the administration. I am not of that mindset. I believe they are intent on "waging war" against us for fear of what we will find. If they remove us from asking questions, then they don't have to give answers. However, I am still here doing my job and still working toward that friendly/adversarial relationship balance that was once part of this political beat.

Is this administration so different that it will challenge our democracy? Will this president even last his entire four years? At his first solo press conference he regaled at how his administration was a fine-tuned machine. Well, that machine's cracks are beginning to show. Some wonder if the administration will implode. Will it be patched up or will it continue on a downward spiral until it's beyond repair? Stay tuned as we all watch it unfold, for better or worse. One thing is for sure, we have never seen anything like this before.

PRESIDENTIAL REPORT CARD

Barack Obama B+ (updated)

It was complete, eight years of the Obama Presidency, and now I can give a total grade on race. You can never erase what has been ingrained in our society for hundreds of years. It will not, nor can it, be changed completely in four or even eight years. But after watching presidents for these past twenty years, the previous occupant of the White House worked to make significant strides to turn the tide on the ills of the community. So that is why I give former President Barack Obama a B+. That grade is directly related to his efforts on criminal justice and overhauling law enforcement, especially those facing issues of brutality and racist behavior. Also included in that ranking is his initiative to bring the federal criminal penalties for powder versus crack cocaine from a 100-to-1 ratio to 1-to-1. That effort successfully reduced the disparity to 18-to-1 during the Obama years. Yet, the reason the disparity did not drop further is due to then Senator Jeff Sessions' opposition to a 1-to-1 ratio. At issue, Whites are believed to use powder cocaine while Blacks use crack. The sentencing ratio reflects that stereotype. It is still unfair. (When it comes to a grade of an A for any president, history will make that determination at least ten years following a president's departure from the Oval Office.)

I am not saying Obama did everything right, but he helped people to understand there are problems when it comes to race and there is a difference between "Jamal and Johnny" as he stated in his eulogy for Pastor Clementa Pinckney of Mother Emanuel Church in Charleston, South Carolina. However, the clear disdain for Obama because of his ideas of inclusion and his skin color contributed to the division that has been exacerbated by the heated racially charged rhetoric heard during the 2016 presidential election cycle. We have been, and continue to be, a nation hypersensitive on matters of race. One example that shocked me was a White woman who said "if only Obama were White." I had to stop the woman and remind her that he was carried in a White woman's body and born from her womb.

INTERIM REPORT CARD

Donald J. Trump (incomplete)

The end of Black History Month 2017 was capped off by the Trump administration touching a third rail in the African American community. More-than-skeptical presidents of HBCUs traveled to the new Trump White House in a quest for substantial funding, something they were promised by those who wrangled the group in and outside of 1600 Pennsylvania Ave. No president of the United States had ever funded the institutions in a manner they wanted and hoped for, and this time, they hoped it would be different. Many of the schools are hanging on by a thread financially and some are even teetering on closure.

What it all boiled down to was a visit with staffers who basically said "offer us a plan and we will invest" and then the photo op came. The presidents were invited to the Oval Office for that photo, not realizing that the anticipated funding for the schools was never actually included in the Executive Order. They still remained hopeful. Weeks later after all the upset over the missed opportunity and the dog-and-pony show, the group made it clear that they were looking for a one-time $25 billion offering, full funding of Title III programs (Strengthening Institutions) and funding of Pell Grants for spring, fall, and summer semesters. It turned out that this was little more than a pipe dream as the Trump administration proposed massive cuts to the 2018 domestic budget. For some of the HBCU presidents, it felt like they had been played. They felt bamboozled and hoodwinked.

The hurt over that situation concerning HBCUs is fathomless. Many of these institutions of higher learning were created because of segregation, as Blacks were not allowed to attend schools with Whites. Also, during slavery, it was against the law for Blacks to read and write. So these schools are held in a sacred space for the Black community, as these 105 facilities are one of the largest catalysts for Black middle income status. The understanding of what these schools mean is ever present on all sides of the equation. With great affinity and gratitude for HBCUs, particularly Morgan State University, I contend that HBCUs love you to success.

With just a few days in office, also in February, President Trump wanted to reach out to Black America. He made an attempt, but it was an epic fail with his statements about the late abolitionist and writer Frederick Douglass, a man who on occasion talked with President Lincoln on matters pertaining to slaves. This time, President Trump lost the perfect photo op moment. It was overshadowed by his mention of Frederick Douglass as if he were still alive, a disaster. The table was filled with a group of African American leaders, some very well-known. That same month also included a tour of the new Smithsonian Museum of African American History and Culture where he was taken by the artifacts and the history of Black America.

That trip to the museum took me back to March 12, 2016, when tensions were raw and fights broke out at the Trump for President Rallies and the Chicago rally was canceled because of violence. Then Republican presidential candidate uttered words in front of a predominately White audience that many Blacks felt was code. He said, "We can't have our first amendment rights taken from us. We are people who built this country and made America great."

I asked about that statement as he made it in front of a predominately White crowd as racial tensions were at its height with Black people being kicked and punched at his rallies. When he used the word "we," it confused many. I asked Press Secretary Sean Spicer if Trump meant "White people" when he said "we." Spicer immediately retorted with a no that is not what he said. But many Blacks saw it differently. They felt it was code then and even now. When you talk with many of his supporters, the contrast in attitudes is totally different. At least publicly, they will tell you it meant all of America. The question still lingers as news organizations from agencies that promote all types of hate are now showing up at the White House as if to be validated. It is the people's house and who am I to censor who comes and goes, but this can only lead to bad things.

The president has made a call for unity, but what does that look like? How will he begin the process? When the hurt is deep, you can't just say words after the pain was inflicted at some of the deepest levels. The pain continues to come via his supporters and their rage against inclusion, the budget cuts that heavily affect minorities and the underserved, and the acknowledgment of certain groups now in the press briefing room with the rest of us. Where do we go from here?

So for now, number 45, President Donald J. Trump, gets an incomplete grade for his efforts on race. If I were to assign a grade, it would not be pretty. I want to be fair and give him and his administration a chance to prove and redeem themselves on matters of race—from healing the divide, to policing, to the travel ban, to fixing HBCUs as promised, to his inner-city fix and so much more. As a reporter, President Trump, I am recording you for history. As a Black woman who understands her history and the history of Blacks in the country, understanding that everyone is not in the same place but realizing I am my brother's (and sister's) keeper, I am waiting on you to help heal the land.

What will you do and how will you do it, if at all?

INDEX

Black farmers, 16–17, 86–87, 134–35, 137

Black media. *See* specialty media

Blacks, 4, 26, 54; American experience of, 5–6, 13–14; employment of, 126, 143; in middle-class, 112–13; political voice of, 25; poverty and, 68–69, 82; recognition of, 36–38; southern culture of, 106–7; White House and, 7–8, 20, 85; Whites and, 5, 11–12

Black soldiers, 21, 34–37, 65, 94. *See also* veterans, Black

Black vote, 70–71, 76, 90–91, 120–21, 123

A Black Woman's Experience: From Schoolhouse to White House (Dunnigan), 7

Blair, Tony, 100

bloggers, 52, 53

bombing, 98

Bosnia, 74

Boyd, John Jr., 17, 86–87

Briefing Room, 31, 41–42, 61, 96

Brown, Ron, 50, 83

budget, 136–37

Bush, George H., 21, 70

Bush, George W., 23, 24, 41, 89, 105, 122; Africa and, 100–101, 102–4; Black community and, 90–91, 104, 141; Clinton, Bill, and, 77, 83, 91–92; faith of, 93, 113; foreign aid and, 100–101; Hurricane Katrina and, 107–11; Iraq War and, 93–94; Kenyan president and, 55–58; Obama and, 25, 111–13; race and, 92, 95–96, 99, 107–8, 145; racial gaff of, 55–59; as vice president, 33–34

Bush, Laura, 100, 105–7, 110, 113

Bush Africa Initiative, 103

Cambridge, Massachusetts, 127–28

cancer, cervical, 103

Cape Town, South Africa, 19

Carter, Jimmy, 69, 71

Case, Carroll, 21

CBC. *See* Congressional Black Caucus

Census Bureau, U.S., 68, 143

change, 8, 10, 71–72, 79

children, 138, 139–40

Christian Evangelicals, 101

CIA leak-gate, 57–58

civil rights, 125; activist, 17, 134–35; movement, 64–65, 67, 109; Obama and, 137; organization, 134–35

Civil Rights Act, 65–66, 67, 99–100

Civil Rights Division, 125

Civil Rights Summit, 81

Clinton, Bill, 7–8, 122; Africa and, 14, 17–19; apology and, 15–16, 17–20, 22, 79–80, 83, 85; Black community and, 81–82, 84–85, 87, 88, 118, 141; Bush, George W., and, 77, 83, 91–92; disappointments of, 85–86; as "first Black president," 22, 82, 84, 118; Gore and, 92–93; Harlem and, 73–74; Jones and, 34; presidential recognition and, 47–48, 49–50; race and, 15, 21, 22–23, 75, 79–80, 88, 145; as "rock star," 74; veterans and, 35–36

Clinton, Hillary, 16, 19, 50, 102, 116, 149–51

Clyburn, James, 5, 66, 82, 120

A Colored Man's Reminiscences of James Madison (Jennings), 3

Comedy Central, 134

Communications Office, 54

complexion, 6, 11

Confederacy, 11–12, 12–13

Congressional Black Caucus (CBC), 14, 69–70, 94, 115–16, 143

Conservative Political Action Conference (CPAC), 150

conservatives, 71, 75, 92, 96, 101

INDEX